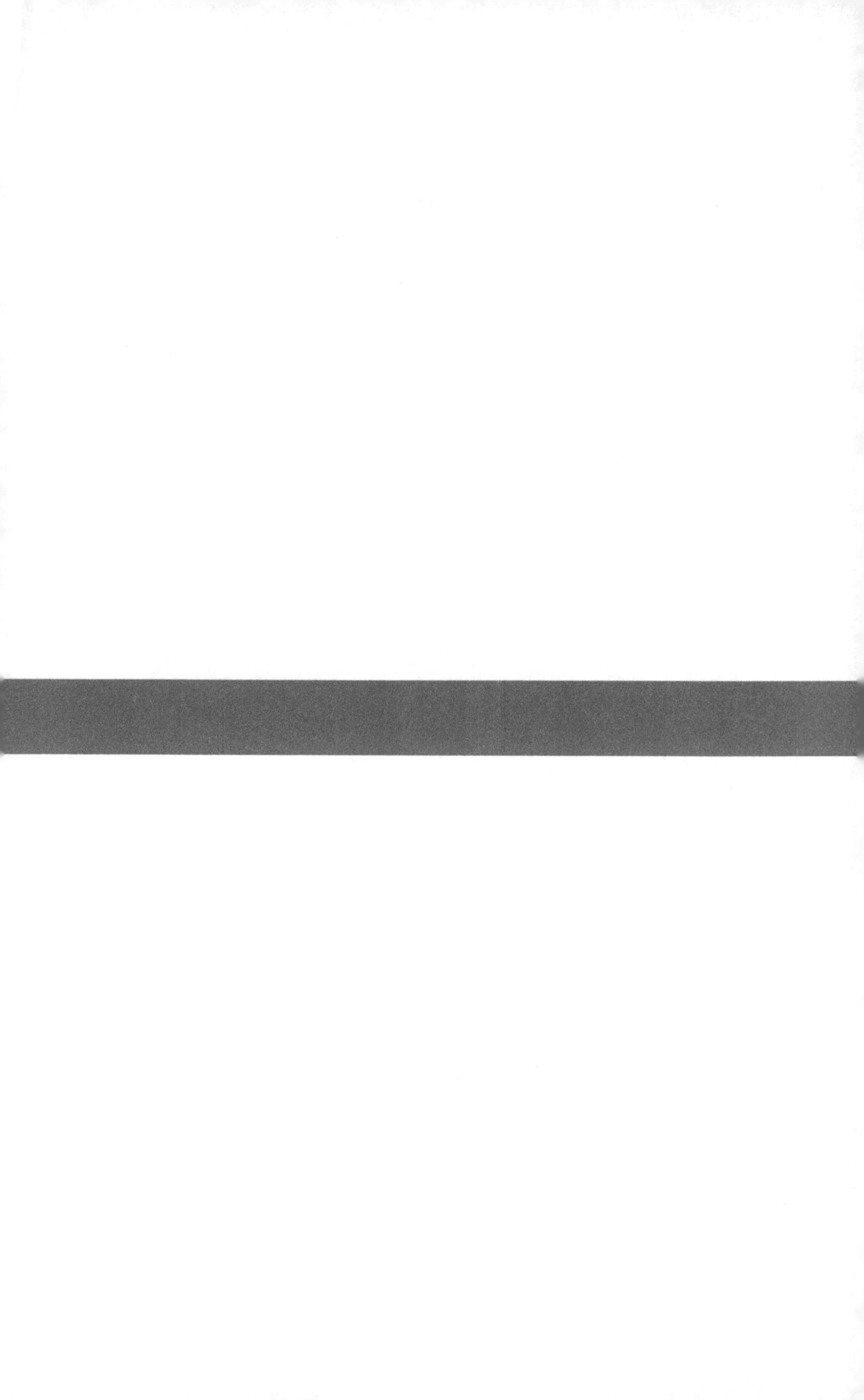

# Gaucho Dialogues on Leadership and Management

# Gaucho Dialogues on Leadership and Management

ALFREDO BEHRENS

ANTHEM PRESS

Anthem Press
An imprint of Wimbledon Publishing Company
*www.anthempress.com*

This edition first published in UK and USA 2018
by ANTHEM PRESS
75–76 Blackfriars Road, London SE1 8HA, UK
or PO Box 9779, London SW19 7ZG, UK
and
244 Madison Ave #116, New York, NY 10016, USA



*British Library Cataloguing-in-Publication Data*
A catalogue record for this book is available from the British Library.

ISBN-13: 978-1-78308-710-5 (Hbk)
ISBN-10: 1-78308-710-2 (Hbk)

This title is also available as an e-book.

I dedicate this book to my teachers and students, through whom I have learned so much; to my wife Luli, who inspired the book and saw me through its creation; and to my children Jimena Camila Cecilia and Pedro, hoping their lives will be led by truth and loyalty, even when it might not pay in the usual mercenary sense.

... he welcomes us,
with a deep, wise and hard silence
that displays an old truth,
strength lies only within us.[1]

[1] Translation of a fragment of the last stanza of Mario Benedetti's poem, *The Leader and His Men* (El Baquiano y los suyos; Benedetti, 2001, 112).

# Contents

# Preface to the English Edition

Ever since Plato discovered that the best way to record the brilliance of the philosopher Socrates was to set down his teacher's imaginary conversations in the Academy, conversational question and answer has been humankind's primary teaching tool. Over the millennia, Socratic Dialogue has been celebrated, reinvented, deconstructed—even lampooned—in a long tradition stretching back through Monty Python, Samuel Beckett, Laurence Sterne, Isaac Walton, Shakespeare and others.

But Alfredo Behrens's timely book must surely represent a new landmark in this ever-growing dialectical genre of "Socratic variations." His mission is to advance our cultural understanding of Latin America and the home-baked spirit of its business and political leadership models, by means of the imaginary dialogues of two fictional heroes from the pampas. They are cowboys who in these parts are named Gauchos. If you want to name their style, you might call it "magical realism meets management theory." Yet *The Gaucho Dialogues* is more than a study of organizational behavior, seen through a Latino lens. It hitches a ride on literature and history too.

The first intention of the writer—an academic teaching business leadership—may be to lay bare the reasons why empirical Anglo-Saxon management methods seem so often doomed to failure when adopted south of the Rio Grande. Yet—most intriguingly for our own times—the writer uses Latin America as a chilling case study in how nationalist, right-wing populism can take root and corrupt any society. He shows too, how political leaders everywhere can seize and hold power by appealing to darker emotional forces driving voters. So this critical examination of Latin America's political foundations—which have made this region both the *alma mater* and "patient zero" of destructive populism—is doubly relevant in an age in which voters in Northern Hemisphere democracies have begun to greedily devour these very same ideas.

Behrens brings to life Martin Fierro—all mustachioed *machismo*, knife-wielding bravura and homespun wisdom from the campsite—by pillaging the eponymous 1872 work of José Hernández, Argentina's poet laureate of Gaucho culture. Fierro's less fiery counterpart and imaginary interlocutor is the more educated Don Segundo Sombra, a literary figure created half a century later by Ricardo Güiraldes, also an Argentine writer who but for his untimely death might have achieved the status of an Hispanic Rudyard Kipling.

Mounted on horseback, these two embark on a jazzy, 200-page riff on the nature of leadership. It is an airy, playful construct showing blatant disregard for that other lynchpin of classical thought: Aristotle's unity of time and place. As they ramble across the historical and metaphorical landscape of the South American continent, the two heroes of this book—Fierro and Sombra—slip effortlessly through time and space. The book weaves its conversational path from the exploits of Argentina's founding dictator Juan Manuel Rosas in the 1830s, all the way to the World War II campaigns of General Patton. Rebellion, slavery, honor and loyalty all make their appearance in this analysis of what makes great leadership.

One moment they are observing the Italian liberator Guiseppe Garibaldi cutting his revolutionary teeth with a ragamuffin band of Neapolitan rebels during the 1842–48 defence of Montevideo. Next they are tracing the origins of Argentinian caudillo Juan Perón's populist style in the 1940s. Turn a page or two and the Gauchos are arguing the finer points of 1990s American management theories of transactional or transformational leadership with modern-day social scientists, before plunging into a debate on the origins of charisma and its use in industry. Largely forgotten figures such as Gumercindo Saraiva (Brazil's "Napoleon of the Pampas"), Pancho Villas and General Pershing all make cameo appearances.

But if this mix of ideas sounds too eclectic, too effervescent, or simply too unfamiliar, Behrens builds a solid narrative base by retelling a southern version of an early-twentieth-century story we all know well. This is the extinguishing of the freedom-loving life of the American cowboy out West; the Range Wars and the land grabs triggered by railways and industrialization; the misery of day-laborers in Chicago's meatpacking yards; the funnelling of former agricultural workers into the great industrial plants of modern capitalism; the emergence of modern management techniques designed to squeeze ever more productivity and profit from human beings.

These same changes—mirrored in social and economic revolutions sweeping through South America's flatlands—form the darker and more gruesome ballast to this book. For centuries, the economic basis of these lands was the export of salted beef, jerky and meat extracts. The institution that made this possible was the *saladero*, or slaughterhouse and meatpacking station.

Before these institutions evolved into the great mechanized conglomerates such as Anglo Meat Company, Liebig or Fray Bentos, every district across the pampas had its local saladero. It was here that herds of cattle were brought in from the plains of Argentina and Uruguay by wandering horsemen for slaughter; and it was here too that the old freedom-loving, anarchistic lifestyle of the Gauchos collided with the oppressive characteristic of a place of fixed, repetitive, mind-numbing work. It was here that city bosses first learned how to organize and exploit peasant labor, co-opting local leaders to enforce their will. Later they used these same tricks to command politics.

The saladeros have long vanished from the Latin landscape, replaced by car plants, call centers and steel mills, all managed by MBAs from the best universities, using state-of-the-art organizational behavior strategies. Yet Behrens's chilling perception is that deep beneath this superficial modernity there may yet lurk an unreconstructed mindset that harks back to the meatpacking era. This, he suggests, may provide an answer to the unsolved question of why foreign management methods always struggle in Latin America. And why, in terms of national politics, transformational, charismatic paternalists have regularly trumped by-the-book, results-driven pragmatists.

Certainly, Fierro and Sombra argue the point through the book's earlier chapters, returning again and again to questions of loyalty, honor, protection and charisma as the enablers of a traditional paternalist style of business and political leadership. Set against the grim process of modernization is the doomed romanticism of those eternal rebels who—just like the Gauchos Fierro and Sombra—stalked Latin America's political landscape. The two salute those rebel bands of Montoneras, or armed paramilitary groups, that first helped achieve independence from Spain's colonial mastery, before being in turn crushed by the consolidation of new regimes. Yet their spirit lived on in the leftist movements that resisted right-wing military government of the 1970s and 1980s, and reminds us why Latin America still retains its unpredictable, passionate political heart.

The organization and management of rebel groups—so different from national armies—helps explain how they got so far. And why they still offer important lessons for managers shaking their heads at dismal employee engagement surveys and lagging productivity. Just like Pancho Villa confronting General Pershing on his disastrous Punitive Expedition into Mexico in 1916, imagination and audacity will galvanize a tiny rebel band facing the artillery and aircraft of massive superior force.

Yet this book is far from a lament, and it is not without hope. Behrens teaches foreign observers that by looking at Latin America from the right end of the telescope, they too can understand its hidden inner workings. Fundamentally, all Latin American organization of its society, workplace and politics is built around a sense of collective identity, of trust and a feeling of personal belonging. Feedback, reward, recognition, and above all love, are the tools needed.

The first requirement is to stop trying to build systems based on the capacity of individuals—and to start thinking more about the compatibility of people. That erroneous view of Latin America, says Behrens, is derived from:

> business schools in the northern hemisphere, where competencies are more abundant, and where it's easier to find individuals able to build their own teams or to develop group competencies—all in an environment where people don't actually need to like each other.

> Between us (in Latin America), love is necessary. And it takes time to build love.
>
> In Latin America, the key lesson we have learned from the leaders of our political revolutions is that first they built their teams—and only then did they start to develop the competencies required of them.

Behrens—a Uruguayan academic who has lived and taught in Brazil for decades—poses one vital question about informal workplace organization that crystallizes his thought. How could it be that the very same Brazilian factory workers considered by MBA-trained managers to be terminally feckless, unproductive and disorganized, would willingly dedicate their spare time to moving mountains, as energetic and accomplished masters of planning and execution for Rio de Janeiro's spectacular Carnival parade?

For eleven months of every year, each of Rio's twenty-odd samba schools mobilizes a 5,000-strong army of unpaid and largely unrecognized volunteers executing tasks every bit as complex as launching a NASA moonshot. No wonder Behrens today works with Rio's *carnavalescos* to teach—or rather *unteach*—senior managers from Latin America's elite business schools, how to interact more constructively with their own workforce. And that is just the tip of the iceberg. Across Latin America, literally millions of people work without pay, largely without recognition and wholly without external organization, by joining in voluntary organizations that work miracles. They bring in the harvest, raise barns, dig wells and take care of each other because they love it. Mobilizing that spirit would, hints Behrens, do much to transform and stabilize the region, freeing it from its lingering status as America's backyard.

So the very simple message of this book is a call for love and respect. Yet only a respected academic with a University of Cambridge PhD, a string of HBR publications and a sophisticated command of the literature (this book's bibliography and footnotes show Behrens is familiar with the canon of management theory, social science and leadership studies), could make such a startlingly naïve-sounding plea to every manager who fancies himself (herself) a true leader:

> You can't manage a company if you don't respect people. They simply won't work for you. And that is why it's crucial to any effective leadership that the person in charge must show coherence of speech and action.

Neither Martin Fierro nor Don Sugundo Sombra ever existed. Today, even the real gauchos are gone, and so are the saladeros. Cattle herds no longer roam free and the rumbustious Montonera spirit has been absorbed into the mainstream. Yet despite this physical absence, something of the old spirit—good and bad—lives on. The customs and underlying behavior patterns of both managers and managed suggest that as modernity sometimes runs only skin-deep, saladeros of the mind can still be found in the darkest corners of South American industry.

So the wisdom of this captivating, good-natured book lies in its understanding that the past—part forgotten, chaotic, violent and turbulent—is the rough canvas that defies attempts to cover it over with smooth layers of corporate paintwork and politically correct speech.

*Richard House*
Former head of FT Confidential (Latin America)

# Preface to the Portuguese Edition

This is a book on leadership and values. It is also a book on beliefs and convictions and their place in one's life.

We are born without a manual of instructions. Each community invents a world and builds in it its own rules and with them attempts to explain life and death and, above all, attempts to explain the self. Each day-to-day affair begs explanation, because no one does anything that is void of meaning to the person. This explained world is what helps find meaning to questions like: Why work? What is the leader's place? What is the follower's place? Which is the model that explains all and renders life livable?

There are many models of explanation and this book explores the Latin American one. It extends the relevance of the author's earlier work, *Culture and Management in the Americas,* adding specificity particularly to the leadership dimension.

To explain leadership, the author finds inspiration in what Latin America has much of: insurrections. Because these often lasted for years and became organizations, insurrections had to solve standard management problems, from translating the leader's vision to executing performance evaluations and securing supply chain.

Alfredo Behrens's explanation resorts to a mythological trip by legendary characters, a trip through a narrated Latin America. The fictional characters, icons of Argentine literature, are two gauchos, Martín Fierro and Don Segundo Sombra. The first is reserved and defiant, the second is reflective and prone to questionings that lead to new perspectives. Both ride on horseback like knights-errant, only to observe and comment rather than taking a quixotic participatory intervention to "right every kind of wrong."

Mythological heroes are no less real than in-the-flesh heroes. All, including the flesh kind, are narrations by others. All of our collective forms—families, cities, nations, continents—are narrations. Alfredo's is a story that attempts to reveal other stories.

Martín Fierro and Segundo Sombra have their own styles of narrating life, which is quite unlike that of pragmatic Benjamin Franklin, for example. These differences point to the need of specific leadership and managerial styles.

The alternative to stillness and serfdom is revolt, but the idea, the perception of a constructive social order, is absent in Fierro. Nonetheless, though Fierro does not have a constructive ethic or a utopian society to dream about, he does have his own beliefs. Fierro's criteria is not geared toward a consequence but is based on his own identity. Similarly, the organizational theorist James March has pointed out that Don Quixote acted not toward an objective but rather in response to his own identity, for "he [Don Quixote] knew who he was."[1]

In the same way, Martín Fierro, observes the most elemental ethics of the survivor, based on immediacy, in contrast with the ethics of his travel partner. Fierro's and Sombra's ethics are not that different, but Sombra is more elaborate and capable of raising questions rather than offering certainties. Fierro's ethic is that of courage; Sombra's is that of prudence. The dialogue between the two elicits much of the discussion that has shaped Latin American management and leadership thinking over past few decades. Fierro epitomizes the strength of xenophobic rebellion underscored by the Latin American penchant for largesse. Behrens attributes to Sombra the vision of saladeros in which workers will be more productive when better led. Yet, to dignity-is-all Fierro, which offers a better death? Where is life better spent, in the gladiator's honorable defeat or in the routine inglorious work in a saladero?

Stories weave meaning, binding reality together, explaining the world. Understanding the stories that circulate in the minds of Latin Americans may lead to understanding a story that would

[1] March and Augier (2004, 176).

otherwise lack any sense; sense would be lacking in any human history of whose underlying founding myths we are unaware.

To lead is to incarnate a story. To build a future is to reckon and shape it. Sarmiento, a contemporary to José Hernandez, used to skewer the gaucho caudillo Facundo by attributing to him a ferocious soul that represented all that was wrong with Argentina. Yet Sarmiento shared Facundo's history and his ferociousness, except instead of making decisions after consulting his horse, Sarmiento rallied the opinions of scientists; instead of dreaming about battles, Sarmiento built schools. Similar passions, different horizons.

Borges told us that only three or four stories lurk in all of humanity's history. Behrens proposes one of them, a mythical trip undertaken by two partners, sufficiently alike as to share but sufficiently different as to make alternative sense of the world they see. In this case, the two partners face a dreamlike trip through Argentina, Uruguay, Brazil, Venezuela, Panama, Costa Rica and Mexico, revealing a fascination with diversity, with teaching indigenous management techniques, and with leadership styles of a continent and offering a metaphor for a permanent, constant matrix that underlies all forms.

Behrens proposes an epistemological trip across the soul of a continent, a trip founded on his own convictions but open enough to reflections on them. In so doing, he offers an opportunity for understanding the difference between dream and reality without suppressing from the dream its potential to shape reality.

*Professor Ernesto Gore*
Former Director
Maestría de Estudios Organizacionales
Universidad de San Andrés
Buenos Aires

# Acknowledgments

I owe much thanks to many since way back to 2010 when I was still just dabbling in this text. Ernesto Gore supported me from its early stages, including by writing the preface to the Portuguese edition of the book. My wife Luli Delgado suggested I turn this work into a story and provided much of the input for Venezuela. Asha Bhandarker and Pritam Singh very thoughtfully mused over the possible relevance of this story in India. Consuelo Adelaida García de la Torre did something similar for Mexico, while Federico Ast did the same for Argentina. Suzy Welch and Jim Darden very kindly commented on earlier versions of this text. Duke Energy commissioned the work in Portuguese to Editora Bei in São Paulo, where Laura Aguiar was a very keen and helpful editor. Once this text saw the light in Portuguese, I have had the benefit of comments from several kind and knowledgeable readers and colleagues at FIA, including Leandro Fraga and former students such as Alexandre Campos and Jonas Marques, as well as from many kind readers who provided generous testimonials.

Many of the comments found their way into this English edition by Anthem Press, where I found enormously talented editorial support to bring this version to its current state, allowing me to appear smarter than I really am. Professor James Wright, Head of FIA business school, kindly authorized funds for the editorial collaboration of Mary Carman Barbosa.

For this Anthem Press edition I wish to thank Richard House for taking the trouble to write a fantastic preface and for helping me to translate the book's meaning to English-speaking audiences.

Everyone helped much to bring this book to this stage and I am very grateful to all.

Publishing a book is akin to throwing a bottle into the sea with a couple of notes in it. You never know what readers might make of it. But I hope they will find in it as much help as I had pleasure in writing it.

Thank you very much.

*Alfredo Behrens*
www.AlfredoBehrens.com

# Introduction

American stories seep into American Management. A goal and a way figure prominently in them. Goals are to be reached with as few resources as possible. Not even time can be wasted, for time is money. Think of *The Wizard of Oz*, Dorothy must follow a yellow brick path to rid herself of her conundrum. "The Little Engine That Could" also had a goal—to carry toys over a mountain, but she could only run on steel rails. Coppola's Captain Willard of *Apocalypse Now* can only chase Coronel Kurtz on a river. Obsessed with killing Moby Dick, Captain Ahab's path to his "fixed purpose is laid with iron rails, whereon [his] soul is grooved to run." The protagonist of *The Old Man and the Sea* must catch a large fish to compensate for the almost three months with no catch, but large fish are in deep waters that can best be reached by sailing straight out from the shore. Even in the Coyote and the Roadrunner cartoons, the Coyote cannot take a shortcut to catch the Roadrunner, the Coyote too must run on a road.

Stories like these nurture the mindset that characterizes American management. But stories differ across the world, leading to different attitudes at work. Where the achievement of goals are not as prevalent, nor the way to reach them so well defined, stories tend to stress conviviality during the journey together, as in a pilgrimage, when reaching the goal is frequently perceived as an anticlimax.

In such societies, usually of a more collectivist bent, working together nurtures the sense of *communitas,* rather than the protagonist ego, rendering less effective much of the American managerial toolkit, such as sought in alignment through individual incentives.

Inasmuch as stories provide us with leading characters of high mimetic value, we will be safe. Safe in the sense that common folk who have decided to act out these behavioral codes will not be in short supply and will be readily recognizable by their willing followers. Both heroes and followers will interact in ways that make it clear to all who is likely to behave as the leader. Once the storm arrives, this highly mimetic character will take the reins in his hands and do what needs to be done. As in Richard Dana's *Two Years before the Mast:*

> I would not wish to have the power of the captain diminished an iota. It is absolutely necessary that there should be one head and one voice, to control everything, and be responsible for everything. There are emergencies which require the instant exercise of extreme power. These emergencies do not allow for consultation.[1]

And the followers will do without hesitation what is expected of them:

> Each one knew that he must be a man, and show himself smart when at his duty.[2]

As a system of societal allocation of talents, this Dana romance would be fine except that it is written by an American author hardly known in Latin America. Because Dana's writings are still read in North American schools, his allusions to living up to one's duty, heroism and obedience still guide people's decisions, helping appoint leaders in organizations, at least in North America.

Does the writing of Latin Americans provide similar tools? To some extent, yes; at the very least, Gaucho-related literature in Argentina, Uruguay and Southern Brazil alludes to similar

[1] Dana (1840, concluding chapter).

[2] Dana (1840, chapter XXIII–"MyWatchmate").

dynamics and performs similar functions. Then there are other local heroes, though seldom related to routine activities such as depicted by Dana.

I leverage my arguments by drawing on the teachings of two fictional protagonists drawn from the gaucho literature: Martín Fierro[3] and Don Segundo Sombra.[4] I chose these two characters because their viewpoints are antipodal to the leadership literature that predominates in the Anglo-Saxon world.

My arguments are put forward through a dialogue between Martín Fierro (Fierro, which means Iron) and Don Segundo Sombra (Sombra, which means Shadow). From a stylistic point of view, I chose to storify the message through a dialogue both a pleasant and effective way of presenting unfamiliar propositions. From an ideological perspective, *Gaucho Dialogues* pays homage to the passionate and reactive nature of Latin Americans, while acknowledging that some of that is responsible for the region's relative technological backwardness.

From the business focus, I blend iconic real and fictional characters as seen from the two main Latin American ideological business perspectives: isolationism and cosmopolitanism. Fierro represents the former, Sombra represents the latter.

Although this book was written mostly with Latin America in mind, its publication has since made an impact in Europe and North America, and to a comparable extent in India, too. Leaders of a populist orientation have challenged the post-war globalist status quo and in some ways they sound of reincarnations of the Martin Fierro type.

Additionally, there is an underlying theme in *Gaucho Dialogues*: the respectful presentation and interpretation of a different culture with its viewpoints, drivers and values. The book shares themes with T. E. Lawrence's *Seven Pillars of Wisdom*[5] or the lighter but no less significant literary contributions of journalist Ryszard Kapuściński, as in *The Soccer War*,[6] *Another Day of Life*[7]

[3] Hernández (2005).
[4] Güiraldes (1926).
[5] Lawrence (1922).
[6] Kapuściński (1992).
[7] Kapuściński (2001).

or *The Shadow of the Sun.* Lawrence's writing reflects the guilt of an honest military officer handling British duplicity in dealing with Arab tribes bound by honor and loyalty, similar to dealings of Latin American work teams. Kapuściński narrated, mostly for the Polish, coups and wars in Latin America and Africa, with their honorable, frightening, and at times grotesque and farcical dimensions.

Fierro and Sombra roam the North through popular revolts in nineteenth- and early-twentieth-century Uruguay, Brazil, Venezuela, Panama, Costa Rica and Mexico. Popular revolts can be considered "organizations" in that they have a leader who needs to communicate a vision in order to recruit and achieve a goal. During the process, the organization must evaluate performance, promote or expel members, and secure the logistics to fulfill the organizational purpose. As such, popular revolts are organizations and have the benefit of having been autochthonous, therefore revealing how people in Latin America preferred to manage themselves before they were distracted by American Scientific Management.

Martín Fierro is the quintessential Argentine gaucho brought to us by José Hernandez in 1872. Don Segundo Sombra is a Kiplinesque gaucho character developed by Ricardo Güiraldes more than half a century later.

In this book, Sombra and Fierro meet and begin together a long journey through much of Latin America, along which they engage in a reflection on leadership and management. Because they are fictional, they are not bound to time and place and can witness popular revolts without interfering in them. They are not bound to realism and therefore are not constrained by it. I use real events to discuss their theories from various viewpoints, which I attribute to both gauchos. Through the characters, I illustrate two contrasting ideological viewpoints in Latin America: the passionate but xenophobic viewpoint represented by Martín Fierro, and the quieter cosmopolitan viewpoint represented by Don Segundo Sombra.

There is no need for the hero to have lived; I think it is fair enough to create a fictional character as long as he has a Frye-realistic touch to it. I rely on stories with archetype-like constructs, to help define what people expect, identifying the shared backdrop that orchestrates our behavior and facilitates communication and teamwork.

Take José Hernández's epic poem, *The Gaucho Martín Fierro* (1872), for instance. The protagonist is a fictional gaucho, father and husband, who in the mid-nineteenth century was forcibly drafted by the army to protect the Argentine Western frontier. Among other vexations, he was forced to work for no pay for the battalion's commander. Martín Fierro chose to desert the army, and upon returning to his *terroir* he realized his wife had not waited for him and that his two children had also moved on. Martín Fierro turned into a hoodlum, provoking duels at bars, during one of which he killed a black man. Fierro thus becomes an assassin as well as a defector and a hoodlum. He must escape. He was spotted and surrounded by a pack of soldiers, led by Sergeant Cruz, who had been sent to capture Fierro; but he resists his imprisonment with such courage as to inspire Sergeant Cruz to betray his army and fight on Fierro's side. Both escape to Indian encampments where, a couple of years later, ultimately Cruz dies in an epidemic and Fierro returns to the outskirts of the city. Upon his return, told in the second book called *The Return of Martín Fierro* (1879), Fierro is now a tamer gaucho. He will measure his responses to provocations; he will be more reflexive, more mature, perhaps the same gaucho only with cleaner fingernails, as Borges would have him.

There is no need to seek an episode that is particularly heroic in Martín Fierro's rendition, because Fierro is a hero at all times. In the best Campbell mythic tradition, Fierro departed, overcame his ordeals, and returned transformed. He is now bound to stand for his rights against anyone; he is free, insubordinate, unbounded, unsettled. These qualities also make him dangerous, because he is susceptible.

José Hernandez's *Martín Fierro* was an immediate success. More than 50,000 copies of his rhymed poem were sold and played on the guitar at rural bars to illiterate gauchos. Yet the urbanite resistance to uncivilized gauchos would have prevailed had not *Martín Fierro* been elevated to its current prominence as Argentina's foundational poem by Leopoldo Lugones, an ultimately conservative and prized Argentine writer. Lugones gave preeminence to Martín Fierro when traditionalist Argentines felt under attack by the hordes of immigrants who could not share in the rural traditions of Argentina.

Martín Fierro lacks the consciousness of the common good, something that may guide him and constrain him toward a strategy. Martín Fierro will not fight for justice, freedom or other such higher causes, unless they are his own. In this sense, Martín Fierro's stance cannot be compared to the heroism of a Costa Rican Juan Santamaría, who offered his life against a foreign invader and preserved Costa Rican identity. In Martín Fierro's behavior there is no abnegation, no concept of martyrdom, for the sake of a better world. What makes Fierro admirable is his disposition to fight for his beliefs, however rudimentary they may be. Borges rightly "argues that Fierro was born to an ethic of courage, not of forgiveness."[8]

I pay tribute to this earthy attitude of Martín Fierro in Chapter 7, where I have an inflamed Fierro explaining to Sombra what Fierro perceives as the beauty of the bullfight.

*Don Segundo Sombra* (1926), on the other hand, is Ricardo Güiraldes's elegy to a legendary gaucho who takes it upon himself to tutor a young man, Fabio Cáceres, in the skills and ethics of a gaucho. In this sense, Sombra is a Kiplinesque counterpoint to Martín Fierro. Sombra is more prudent, less eloquent and more reserved than Fierro is portrayed. In taking on the role of tutor to a younger, fatherless man, Sombra is more giving and has a greater sense of future and building than the ever-fighting Fierro.

Güiraldes died soon after the book was published and Güiraldes's Sombra took longer than José Hernández's Fierro to be assimilated by the Argentine public; it can be rightly argued that Sombra never acquired the stature of Fierro as an Argentine iconic character. Nonetheless, they are complementary and I use both viewpoints, Fierro's and Sombra's, to assess the leadership and management instances they face on their journey.

There is an underlying thread in my story: the search for a father in a patriarchal society. In Latin America as a whole, the share of contemporary households led by females is about double that of the United States. Accordingly, the fatherly education of

[8] Borges (2005, 110).

their own children plays little or no role for either Martín Fierro or Don Segundo Sombra.

Mexican Juan Rulfo's *Pedro Páramo* has the book's leading character, Luciano Preciado, searching for his father. Colombian Gabriel Garcia Marquez's *Love in the Time of Cholera* has the leading character, Florentino Ariza, acting as the author's own elusive father. I would dare say that, throughout the continent, the cry for an absent father may underscore the strength of a mythical paternalist style of leadership.

I close the saga with the stark comparison of Fierro and Sombra to American war hero, General Patton, and his strong role in the education of his own children, suggesting that Latin America needs to correct its current lack in parental upbringing in order to give their children the education required to build more modern societies.

The book is structured in chapters that follow the revolts. In chapter 1 the characters and the setting are introduced. In chapter 2 Fierro and Sombra consider Fierro's own influence over General Perón's leadership style. In chapter 3 Fierro and Sombra discuss the role of honor in defiance, as in the gladiator's motivation to fight. In chapter 4 the two riders assess leadership and management in the long siege of Montevideo (1843–51), particularly the role of Giuseppe Garibaldi. They then discuss, in chapter 5, leadership and management theory as received from the north. In chapter 6 the characters continue northward into southern Brazil and are again exposed to a combatant grassroots movement, and witness the Federalist revolt (1893–95). From there they move to Venezuela where in chapter 7 they discuss the mythical significance of bullfighting and mostly witness, in chapter 8, the Marcha Restauradora and the Presidencies or otherwise tutelages of Cipriano Castro and Juan Vicente Gómez (1899–1935). Fierro and Sombra continue northwards and in chapter 9 they witness the secession of Panama from Colombia (1903) and move on to Costa Rica to discuss the role of drummer Juan Santamaria in preserving Costa Rican identity from aggression by American filibuster William Walker (1856). In chapter 10 Fierro and Sombra become acquainted with the Mexican Revolution, witness the battle of Zacatecas (Mexico, 1914) and discuss the leadership styles of the various protagonists in the Mexican Revolution and, in chapter 11, the ensuing Punitive Expedition led by General "Black Jack" Pershing (1916–17) and they draw a comparison with American General Patton and West Point as a school of discipline, war and permeability to innovation, despite its stress on military obedience. The book ends with an epilogue as a summary of the lessons gathered and a counterpoint between spontaneous charismatic leadership and the taming of discipline of West Point, as expressed in General Patton.

All things considered, *The Gaucho Dialogues* proposes espousing modernity grounded in core regional values, suggesting ways of tailoring management and leadership to a tribal people. In this sense, the book may also be relevant to management in many other regions of the world, where—as in Latin America—people hold tribal values more dearly than in the Anglo-Saxon world. where much of today's leadership and management theory comes from.

As much as management practitioners and academics would benefit from reading Lawrence and Kapuściński, the same managers or scholars could benefit from reading *The Gaucho Dialogues,* with the additional benefit of the writing being closer to their managerial interest; particularly at a time when a graduate of one of the earliest American business schools considers it appropriate to wall in the country and manage the world out from there.[9]

[9] At the time of this publication, American President Trump, a Wharton business school graduate, is in the first year of his mandate.

# 1

# Fierro and Sombra Head for Mexico

It was dusk and the gauchos had called it a day's work. They had herded cattle for a good thirty miles that day. Only another morning would be enough to complete the journey. Campfires were springing up here and there. The legendary Martín Fierro was sitting alone at one, sipping mate while some skewered pieces of beef were roasting nearby. Don Segundo Sombra approached Martín Fierro, "Good evening, Fierro!" Without raising his gaze Fierro invited Sombra to join him. "Come closer Don Segundo, you may come closer." Now at greater ease, Sombra walked more swiftly toward Fierro. "You know me, Fierro?" Drawling his words, Fierro would tease him, "I can tell a lazy one."

"Ah, Fierro! You will never quit your defiant style!" Sombra scoffed at Fierro's provocation and Fierro invited him further, "Come closer, Don Segundo, unless it is to ask something from me." Sitting down by Fierro's campfire, Sombra continued, "I am not here to ask, Fierro, but to invite you."

The differences in the behavioral styles of both gauchos were well known: Fierro was a provocateur, quick to draw his deadly *facón* at half-a-chance, while Sombra was more Kiplinesque, known to have mentored the young Fabio, whose cattle they were now herding to a Buenos Aires slaughterhouse to be salted to produce jerked beef mostly for export. "Why would Don Segundo Sombra invite a humble gaucho like me?" asked Fierro, "if through Fabio you are closer to the buyers of the cattle we herd?"

Sombra pulled the stem of Pampa grass and placed it into his mouth to feel it's reassuring sour, earthy taste, on which gauchos had long relied for orientation, and explained his visit, "I came to invite you to a chat. This gaucho business is coming to an end. We can already see the lights of Buenos Aires. Tomorrow we will hand over the cattle, and we will get paid. What shall we do afterwards, Fierro?"

Fierro took his time to reply, he took his last three strong sips from his mate gourd until it made its characteristic noise announcing it was empty. He filled the gourd again and offered it to Sombra, speaking in a lower tone, "You are wiser than I am, Sombra. You had that child Fabio to bring up. Mine were already grown when I saw them again, after being forcibly drafted; by then they were prone to listen to the advice of Vizcacha, the scoundrel." In a strident voice Fierro now imitates Vizcacha:

> Whatever you do, keep in with the Judge,
> what he says, store well in mind;
> if he starts to get angry, drop your head;
> don't get in his way while he's seeing red;
> a paling to rub your ribs against
> is a comfort, you'll often find. (Owen, 1936, 197)

"Tell me, Sombra, is that advice you should give a young man? The devious values of the city are taking over, Sombra!" Fierro went on, "It's the end, Sombra. The foreigners are setting up barbed wire all over. It's becoming impossible to be a gaucho."

In fact, Fierro was right; with the expansion of agriculture, the land was being fenced and cattle herding was quickly becoming a nuisance to the system. The free, nomadic lifestyle of the gaucho was coming to an end.

Sombra confirmed Fierro's conclusion that their lifestyle was over.

"It's the same everywhere. I taught Fabio a few things, but he cannot be altogether himself. He must sell his cattle to the saladero."

"Hideous work, Sombra!"

"Yes, Fierro, at saladeros cattle are slaughtered and the beef jerked, providing the mainstay to the population."

"Some life!"

"Yes, Fierro. The low-technology, routine work of salting meat is a metaphor for the workers at saladeros salting themselves out of life, leading to a style of production that would later evolve into the large industrial beef conglomerates and other business."

"What is life like in a saladero, Sombra?"

"More than a hundred people work there. For every five of them there is a boss."

"All telling you what is to be done, Sombra?"

"Yes, Fierro, at the saladero there are big bosses and small bosses. There is no freedom there! It's one stepping on another's tail! He who steps on more tails has a more privileged position."

"Nobody would step on my tail, Sombra!"[1]

"I know that, Fierro. A century from now we will have Professor Gore warning the likes of us about thirty-one ways of pretending to collaborate in the saladeros without really doing so."[2]

"Thirty-one ways? Holy God! That's worse than even Vizcacha ever mustered!"

"Yes, and it will only get worse; Vizcacha was only an apprentice, Fierro. There," pointing to the saladero, "the judge will be befriended by the saladero boss and his business will be guaranteed. The saladero's survival will be guaranteed. Little bosses will be complacent with their superiors and inconsiderate with their subordinates."

"Cowards!" yelled Fierro.

"And that is only one of Gore's thirty-one ways to behave like a coward, Fierro!"

"Tell me another one, Sombra!"

"Be a follower, because the responsibility will remain with the leader!"

"Good gracious me, Sombra! Nobody draws the facón to straighten matters there? Is everybody dead at the saladeros?"

"They are Fierro, but they do not know it yet. Vizcacha won, Fierro. The Devil won!" said Sombra as he crossed himself, and continued, "But let's go north, Fierro, we will have more room for

[1] See stanzas 11–13 of *El Gaucho Martin Fierro* for an illustration of Fierro's defiant attitude (Hernández, 2005).

[2] Gore (2009).

ourselves there. They are still at war against each other over there, Fierro; they have no time for barbed wire fences."

Looking at the ground, Fierro replied, "I think I will join you and search for my father."

"Do you have a father?"

"Don't we all?"

"I mean; do you know your father?"

"Not me, my mother did though."

"And what became of him?"

"He returned to Mexico."

"Mexico?"

"Yes, to Comala. He left Mexico for Peru. Ended up in Tucuman, through Potosi. In Tucuman he met my mother."

"And what was his name?"

"Pedro Páramo."

"Are you related to Luciano Preciado, his son?"

"The same father!"

"Are you sure your mother knew him?"

In one swift gesture, Fierro left his mate gourd on the soil, placed his right hand on his facón, rolled his *chiripá*[3] onto his left forearm, and shouted at Don Segundo Sombra:

"Are you suggesting my mother would lie to me, Sombra?"

"Take it easy, what's going on Fierro?"

"Are you suggesting my mother did not know my father? That she was a whore? Do you believe that? Hold your ground if you dare!"

"That is not what I meant, Fierro!"

But Fierro would no longer listen. Defiantly he continued, "Repeat it if you are a macho!"

"Calm down, Fierro!"

"Calm down my foot! Repeat it if you are a macho! Repeat it!" yelled Fierro as he advanced onto Sombra, who would not reach for his own facón. Fierro corners Sombra against a carriage, took him by his neck, and held his facón onto Sombra's belly.[4]

[3] The *chiripá* is a traditional piece of gaucho trousers. It consists of a worsted shawl with a corner drawn between the legs and tucked over the lace pantaloons.

[4] Honor, and the personal violence to which it gives place, has been part of the region's ethos since inception. Its roots may be Mediterranean and the

"Calm down, Fierro! We both are already dead! Are you forgetting that? You can't kill me again!"

Fierro relaxed his muscles, pulled back his facón from Sombra's belly, let Sombra's neck go, and took a step back.

Don Segundo continued, "I am a macho, Fierro, and you know it, though I never fought for anything I did not need to. I grew out of killing. And you?"

"I did not kill, Sombra! I only defended my space! Nobody ever set foot into it to bother me and left on his two legs. Who set foot and was not my friend ended up with a stab in his guts."

"Sombra, I think that if God wanted me in this world it was not to be injured or listen to insults. I believe God tests my worthiness of being here when I fight, on this grass, not lying under it. I know that when my time arrives it will be the other man's facón digging into my guts; he will be closer to my mother, and to hers, and to God in that way. But I will have died defending my dignity, which is all I have, and which is the last thing a man should loose. It is that simple, Sombra!"

"What for, Fierro?"

"So that I would die in peace, Sombra."

"Killing, Fierro?"

"I already told you I did not kill. They were going to die in any case. They were only asking for a shove to put an end to their purposelessness. I only pushed them a little. That was it."[5]

"For nothing, Fierro?"

"It is never for nothing, Sombra. I like to fight. It makes me feel good. I feel closer to God."

"When feeling closer to death, Fierro?"

"No, Sombra. When I fight I do not feel death. I feel the limit of the other's life." Fierro then mimicked a fighting stance, spread his feet apart, and threw his body forward with his armed right hand extended and shouted, defiant, "He made it up to here! To the point of my facón. When I penetrate into his belly button I feel closer to his mother, and to his mother's mother, mothers

narration of this particular event is inspired by a knife duel at a bar brawl in Greece (Gallant, 2002, 359–82).

[5] See stanzas 18–19 in *El Gaucho Martín Fierro* for an illustration of Fierro's remorseless attitude (Hernández, 2005).

all the way back! This is how I feel closer to God, and I feel closer to God the more the other one defends himself. Killing the other is a sublime moment in one's life, Sombra!"

"It may be, Fierro, but why?"

"We are all doomed to die, Sombra! When one kills the other we have secretly triumphed, temporarily, but we have triumphed."

"Elias Canetti will one day say something along those lines, Fierro."

"He might have me in mind then, Sombra. I only want to win fast, to vindicate my mother's tears and all promises broken by men. But I also love the stench of the other's fright, the taste of his sweat, his desperate cries, the heat, the tensioned muscles; all inflames me as if even the wind would draw me against the other body to dig my facón into his guts, because it was God's will to be like that. Otherwise it would be his facón into my belly. God has his ways; this is why it has always been me, not them, so far."

"You will also fall like all have fallen in pursuit of vanity, Fierro; so said Shakespeare in his *Macbeth.*[6] But did God want you to approach your opponents in that way?"

"God never told me how, Sombra. I think that if God wanted me in this world it was not to be injured or listen to insults. I believe God tests my worthiness of being here when I fight, on this grass, not lying under it. I know that when my time arrives it will be the other man's facón digging into my guts; he will be closer to my mother, and to hers, and to God in that way. But I will have died defending my dignity, which is all I have, and which is the last thing a man should loose. It is that simple, Sombra!"

"It may be so, Fierro. But it sounds like a waste of life! Or even a life told by a player fretting in his hour of glory.[7] In any case, what is to be done between fights, Fierro?"

"I don't know, Sombra. I had no time to ask myself that question. It has been one long struggle for me. There are men who know about those things. They know how to fight and know how to

[6] "And all our yesterdays have lighted fools / The way to dusty death. Out, out, brief candle" (Shakespeare, c1606, *Macbeth,* Scene 5, 22–23)

[7] "Life's but a walking shadow, a poor player / That struts and frets his hour upon the stage/And then is heard no more: it is a tale / Told by an idiot, full of sound and fury" (Shakespeare, c1606, *Macbeth,* Scene 5, 24–27).

do things. Rosas was one of them, Sombra. But you see what happened. City people teamed up with the Neapolitans who didn't even know how to mount on horseback. Together they fenced all the land with barbed wire, making our lives hell when we want to herd cattle. Argentina is no longer a land for gauchos, Sombra!"[8]

"Argentina might no longer be, Fierro, this is why I invite you to move north. But let me warn you Fierro; nativism quickly spills into excess. Even in the cradles of liberalism we will see shallow, xenophobic, calls for nativism in the early twenty-first century."

"Let's go. Sombra. Fear not, we are both dead, remember?"

"I do not fear losing, Fierro. I want to learn and teach, that is all."

"Then let us leave tomorrow morning, Sombra! Let's leave and you can teach me whatever you want. I'm going to search for my father."

"Right, Fierro! Tomorrow morning, we depart for Mexico. The trip has begun!"

[8] See stanzas 23–35 and following of *El Gaucho Martin Fierro,* for an illustration of Fierro's musings on better times, particularly his lament on stanza 35 (Hernández, 2005).

# 2

# The Unquenchable Thirst for Honor: The Gladiator

> "Perhaps Spartacus wondered how he could defeat hopelessness, but still he must have found compensation, even exultation, in defying the odds of his existence that entailed an inevitable degradation. Seen under this light, much of the unlawful behavior of our urban youth in drug trafficking is akin to the behavior of the gladiators!"

Early in the morning, Fierro and Sombra decamped and leisurely led their horses to cross the River Uruguay; the ride will take a few days during which they will exchange views on several subjects. The first exchange is on dueling.

"Fierro, you enjoy dueling. You could have been a gladiator."

"Perhaps I was one, Sombra."

"Tell me, then, Fierro, because you sound as if you had been there. Why did a gladiator fight at all? For he, or she, in being originally a slave, would be seen as less than a follower, certainly not a leader, therefore fit only for dying, tomorrow if not today. Why, then, would they fight at all?"

"The gladiator was not wholly deprived of dignity, Sombra. Even more telling, his dignity was reckoned by the audience who had power of life and death over him."

"Would you say, Fierro, that more dignity was bestowed upon the gladiator then than today's societies are willing to bestow upon many of its workers at the saladeros?"

"I think so, Sombra. Think, if you wish, of the hordes of workers hauled into the saladeros every morning. What dignity is conceded to those people who toil, as they do in Rio de Janeiro, São Paulo or Mexico, three to four hours a day in transportation alone, and in such appalling conditions! Only to earn a pittance after a full day's work, and only to reignite the ritual the next day?”

“But Fierro, more frequently than not, the gladiator is today seen as a slave forced to fight for his life. We rightly wonder, why would he bother to fight at all if his life were so miserable? For if continued miseries were the only outcome, why would the gladiator not prefer to die sooner rather than later?”

“Sombra, are the people who work at the saladeros any freer than the gladiators were?[1] What choice do they have? Furthermore, toward the beginning of that era, the majority of the gladiators were volunteers, like the workers at the saladeros today.”

“I think so, Sombra. Think, if you wish, of the hordes of workers hauled into the saladeros every morning. What dignity is conceded to those people who toil, as they do in Rio de Janeiro, São Paulo, or Mexico, three to four hours a day in transportation alone, and in such appalling conditions! only to earn a pittance after a full day's work, and only to reignite the ritual the next day?”

“But Fierro, more frequently than not, the gladiator is today seen as a slave forced to fight for his life. We rightly wonder, why would he bother to fight at all if his life were so miserable? For if continued miseries were the only outcome, why would the gladiator not prefer to die sooner rather than later?”

“Fierro, you are arguing that gladiators chose to be gladiators—perhaps a constrained choice, like that of today's boxers and bullfighters, but a choice nonetheless? But did the gladiators have any choice?”

“Sombra, the gladiators could have been attracted to the game for the game's rewards: the love of glory, the desire to test themselves in life-and-death situations; perhaps they were even attracted to the game by more morbid compulsions.”

“Now, Fierro, you are talking sense. Among the morbid compulsions should we list suicidal proclivities, the desire to taste the killing, perhaps sadism and masochism, too?”

“Sombra, you've read too much! And from an individualist

[1] People are not free unless they can choose (Pesante, 2009, 289–320).

cultural perspective in which the individual's character traits overly dictate his behavior."

"Is it not so, Fierro?"

"Sombra! Let us not forget that the gladiator tournaments were a social event that attracted nobility and gentry, men and women and children alike, and which raised substantial revenue, very much like bullfighting and boxing do today."[2]

"Aha!"

"Sombra, allow yourself to be more daring; what if the gladiator's leitmotif was to perform an act of defiance of hopelessness?"

"Could the gladiator hope to defeat hopelessness, Fierro? Remember the Roman slave Spartacus and the common maps of the lives of six thousand crucified slaves!"[3]

"Perhaps Spartacus wondered how he could defeat hopelessness, but still he must have found compensation, even exultation, in defying the odds of his existence that entailed an inevitable degradation. Seen under this light, much of the unlawful behavior of our urban youth in drug trafficking is akin to the behavior of the gladiators!"

"But, Fierro, unlike in your facón duels, the gladiator was a slave in an arena where he, or even she, would fight for his or her life as though the audience were behind a one-way glass. He can't have found satisfaction in public recognition!"

"The gladiatorial oath, Sombra, was a voluntary debasement of freedom that transformed the gladiator's behavior into the outcome of a contract. Inasmuch as he was a party to a contract, the gladiator's behavior needs no further explanation. A gladiator does what he is meant to do; through the oath, he regained his capacity to be honorable once more. Should the gladiator deny his mandatory behavior as a gladiator, then he would be behaving dishonorably."

[2] Fighting for the entertainment of others has a long evolving story which has left an architectural footprint. from coliseums to stadiums, through arenas (Kyle, 1998, 95).

[3] Defeated slaves were crucified along the 120-mile road from Capua to Rome; the map of their lives, from birth to death, in scripted on their bodies as signposts on a map (Fast, 1951, 251).

"Precisely, Sombra! Public recognition cannot have been the leitmotif. That wisdom is insufficient to explain why the gladiator would fight at all, particularly as the majority were volunteers. The gladiators can no longer be seen as a cultural instance of utter degradation where his or her death was only mockery. There must have been an element of redemption in the game."[4]

"Again, why did a gladiator fight at all, Fierro?"

"Because in Rome, the gladiator's significance was greater than his death; because to Romans, honor was the result of a complex web of self-sacrifice."

"Such as?"

"Devotion, Sombra! Devotion! Remember the ceremonial dedication epitomized by Roman General Publius Decius Mus who in the Samnite Wars (340 BC) offered his body to a violent death by the enemy. Fidel Castro would offer to do the same during the 1962 Missile Crisis, when all Cubans could have been scrapped.[5] The Roman general's behavior was aimed at inspiring the gods to grant victory to his Roman warriors. Similar devotions to death, if less immediate, were seen to be the reason behind the fearlessness of several Roman generals."

"So, Fierro, you are arguing that it was this web of self-sacrifice the gladiators were drawn into, and this was the light under which their performance at fighting would be judged by the audiences?"

"Yes, Sombra. I will not deny that in the beginning the gladiatorial battles were fueled with the bodies of the defeated by Rome. Gladiators were mostly Gauls, Spaniards and Arabs, as well as Thracians and Germans and many more. However, toward the end of the Republic approximately half of the gladiators were volunteers, though the stigma of condemnation lived on in their quarters, food and general living conditions."

"But, Fierro, as you point out, volunteer gladiators came later."

[4] Except for the possibility of escape there was not enough going on for the enslaved gladiators, unless one is willing to admit that they had turned into fighting machines (Barton, 1989, 1–36).

[5] Fidel Castro gave the green light to the Russians to fire their Cuban based missiles first, knowing that the American retaliation would have decimated Cuba (Alloyn, Blight & Welch, 1989, 141).

"But they volunteered attracted by the same reason, Sombra! Remember Cyprianus:

> What is this, I ask you, of what nature is it, where those offer themselves to wild beasts, which no one has condemned, in the prime of life, of comely appearance, in costly garments? While still alive they adorn themselves for a voluntary death, and miserable as they are, they even glory in their sufferings.[6] (Cyprian in *Ad Donatum*, 7).

"The dignification of the gladiator's behavior through the oath turned him into an unstoppable fighting machine, geared toward invincibility. Because he was already dead, the gladiator was now made fearless, for he was compelled to die, but he would die unconquered."

"I see the attraction of the ritual and even the poetry around it, but I still cannot understand why gladiators fought, Fierro!"

"Of course life was tough, Sombra! Of course most gladiators had been debased, but one should not understate the power of the gladiatorial oath, for through the oath the gladiator swore to endure all duress, including finally being slain by the sword."

"You mean to say the gladiator felt bound by an oath that had been ensconced under duress, Fierro?"

"The oath, Sombra, was a voluntary debasement of freedom that transformed the gladiator's behavior into the outcome of a contract. Inasmuch as he was a party to a contract, the gladiator's behavior needs no further explanation. A gladiator does what he is meant to do; through the oath he regained his capacity to be honorable once more. Should the gladiator deny his mandatory behavior as a gladiator, then he would be behaving dishonorably."

"Fierro, you are rewriting history here."

"Sombra, it is you who are interpreting history through the lens of a modern disenchanted man! The role of the gladiators'

[6] Cyprianus, in ad Donatum 7, had already spelled out the significance of dress and appearance in heightening a person's self-perception: "And he who is distinguished by his rich clothes and looks spectacular in his gold and purple, when does he resign himself to wearing common and simple dress?" (Brent, 2010, 48).

"Fierro, you are arguing that Roman culture expected of the gladiator a behavior akin to that of the sacrificial victim, who was led to the altar by a loose rope, not dragged by it. It was even considered a bad omen if the rope tightened, for then the victim was not collaborating with the sacrifice."

"As today it is a bad omen, Sombra, when the inhabitants of the periphery of Rio de Janeiro destroy the train stations and the trains when they arrive late—and full—to the station where they are awaited to take the workers to the saladeros." These workers normally are led to work by a loose rope whose tightening is only occasionally perceived in the anger with which the mob turns against the transport medium that enslaves them on a day-to-day basis."

oath is like the bondage that was picked up by Alexandre Dumas in *The Count of Monte Cristo,* by having the pirate, whose life the Count did not take in duel, become the Count's slave."

"Therefore, Fierro, you are arguing that the gladiator's behavior cannot be different than what is expected of him. His behavior is shaped by others."[7]

"Precisely, Sombra! It has always been like that! The ancien régime casts a much longer shadow that is usually admitted. Very much like the Duke of Wellington's understanding that his behavior was predetermined when he stated, 'I am the Duke of Wellington, and must do as the Duke of Wellington doth.' "[8]

"Then Fierro, you are arguing that, through the gladiatorial oath, what originally was a slave condemned to death became, if not a free agent, a person with a rightful mandate."

"That is it, Sombra! The dignification of the gladiator's behavior through the oath turned him into an unstoppable fighting machine, geared toward

[7] In a fascinating account of American behaviorist Herbert Simon and Argentine writer Jorge Luis Borges, the latter was interpreting Simon's stance as similar to the power of a god that knowing all of Borges' history, that of his predecessors included, Borges' own behavior could be entirely predicted, for he would not be more than the collection of his behavioral history. I owe this to Professor Ernesto Gore (Primera Plana, 1971).

[8] People may be no more than characters of a play written through history (Thompson, 1990, 9).

invincibility. Because he was already dead the gladiator was now made fearless, for he was compelled to die, but he would die unconquered."

"Is this, Fierro, what came to be recognized as the 'spirit of the gladiator'?"[9]

"Precisely, Sombra! The gladiator is not on a par with his master nor with the audience in front of whom he fights, but fight well he must."

"Like the Marxian proletariat or our men at the saladeros, Fierro? Both are free only inasmuch as to sell the services of their labor."

"That is it, Sombra; you are beginning to get it! The gladiator is not free except to do his duty, and to the fulfillment of his duty there are no limits. Bob Dylan caught the spirit well: 'When you got nothing, you got nothing to lose.'"[10]

"Fierro, perhaps the oath alone was not enough to secure such adherence to the script. Long training and team building must have contributed, too, as well as rewards like the banquet-like dinner the night preceding the game, or the celebration of the game with pomp."

"Indeed, Sombra. All trappings and training led to a most scrupulous observance of the will of the gladiator's master, contributing to the sense of a man of honor. The saladero owners will pick that lesson from Harvard Business School, too!"

"That's it, Fierro! Treat men like pigs and they will behave like pigs! But if you recognize their uniqueness, their dignity, you will get the best out of them."

"You have a point there, Sombra! Trust a man like you to come up with that! Indeed, Sombra, should the gladiator fail to meet his duty he would be dishonored."

[9] This transcends the Roman era and reappeared in St. Augustine's Psalm LXXI as the Gladiatiorium animum; because a gladiator knew he was expected to perish in the next fight if not in the current one, whence the gladiator appears as free as a sinner, no less than Apostle Paul, who turned to God."

[10] In what appears to be the first use of a rock lyric to back a legal proposition in a Supreme Court decision. Chief Justice Roberts aptly quoted Bob Dylan, in Like a Rolling Stone, on Highway 61. Revisited, Columbia Records 1965 (Roberts, 2008).

> "Therefore, Fierro, you argue that, to the gladiator as well as to the bullfighter or the boxer, a good performance produces the audience's pleasure, which bestows upon the actor the honor of recognition. Such is the appeal of the simplicity of splendor unlikely to be achieved outside the arena, or the ring, by those that become gladiators, bullfighters, or boxers?"

"Fierro, you are arguing that Roman culture expected of the gladiator a behavior akin to that of the sacrificial victim, who was led to the altar by a loose rope, not dragged by it. It was even considered a bad omen if the rope tightened, for then the victim was not collaborating with the sacrifice."

"As today it is a bad omen, Sombra, when the inhabitants of the periphery of Rio de Janeiro destroy the train stations and the trains when they arrive late—and full—to the station where they are awaited to take the people to the saladeros. These workers normally are led to work by a loose rope whose tightening is only occasionally perceived in the anger with which the mob turns against the transport medium that enslaves them on a day-to-day basis."

"Yes, Fierro, it is similar behavior. That the gladiator may wish to cooperate in pleasing the audience by putting up a 'good fight' is not normally considered healthy behavior nowadays."

"However, Sombra, think again of Scorsese's *Raging Bull* where, outside the ring, prized boxer Jake LaMotta lives in a circle of deceit and treason."

"What then, Fierro?"

> "That's it, Fierro! Treat men like pigs and they will behave like pigs! But if you recognize their uniqueness, their dignity, you will get the best out of them."

"Sombra, Jake LaMotta's debased existence outside the ring is so demanding that it triggers a life of paranoia, where LaMotta is unsure of his wife's fidelity or even his own brother's loyalty. Only in the ring, Sombra, does Jake LaMotta find respite; for there the rules are known and he knows why he is hitting and being hit.[11] Under those rules a good fight yields honor. Without the basic fighting rules, including the insistence

[11] Martin (1980).

on the gladiatorial mandate to fight an 'equal opponent,' a boxing match would be reduced to mere homicide, which is how gladiator games were perceived when a gladiator failed to perform."

"Therefore, Fierro, you argue that, to the gladiator as well as to the bullfighter or the boxer, a good performance produces the audience's pleasure, which bestows upon the actor the honor of recognition. Such is the appeal of the simplicity of splendor unlikely to be achieved outside the arena, or the ring, by those that become gladiators, bullfighters, or boxers?"

"To those you may add gauchos in a facón duel, Sombra!"

"Fierro, you may be right after all. That may be why nobles and freemen may have approached the arena toward the end of the Republic and the Early Empire. Then, at a time of treachery and debasement, becoming a gladiator may have been a shortcut to earning glory, however fleeting!"

"That's it, Sombra! The life of the gladiator was still considered fit for the debased, even those gladiators freed on account of their performance could not expect to live except at the fringes of Roman society."

"But then, Fierro, free men measuring themselves against a gladiator ought to have been debasing per se. In what sense could the gain to freemen be greater than their eventual loss?"

"Sombra, facing a gladiator was, to some, the opportunity to test themselves against a time-proven truth: Rome's Golden Age lay in the past, in a warrior nation, when the enemy was clear, as was truth. Facing a gladiator may have had a cleansing effect, as later the penitence would to the Catholics."

"You've persuaded me, Fierro. Because, just as the audience held the key to the recognition of the performance on stage, that a nobleman would descend to the level of the gladiator was, to the audience, an assurance that the gladiator's opponent was there for something much greater than usual and that, should he prevail, so much greater would his honor be!"

"Like in facón duels, Sombra! I hate killing a poor bastard that does not know how to hold his ground. But kill him I must!"

# 3

# Martín Fierro Inspires Perón's Leadership Style

> "If Perón lasted too long, it was because he stopped fighting, Sombra!"
>
> "There is some wisdom in your fighting after all, Fierro! It is a tough process to sift leaders, but it surely is an effective one!"

The next dawn was like any other dawn for all, except for Fierro and Sombra. They saddled their horses and continued north, through the Argentine Mesopotamia, crossed the River Uruguay and headed away from Montevideo, under siege by Oribe, a local ally of Argentine Rosas. Oribe was fighting against liberals and foreigners; traitors, according to Fierro.

As they made their way to the River Uruguay, before leaving Argentina, Sombra put Fierro on the spot.

"What do you know about Perón, Fierro?"

"That he was a friend of the people. He was on Rosas side, wasn't he, Sombra?"

"It's disputed, Fierro, but you are right; in many ways he was a modern Rosas. He governed with an iron fist and was supported by the people. Does that make him a hero, Fierro?"

"To most, including me, that does make him a hero, for sure, Sombra. Not to you?"

"I think you may be right, Fierro. In many ways he was like you: proud and defying."

"Nonsense, Sombra. He was much more than I could hope to be. To me, he was educated enough, he had a wife who was admired and loved by all."

"Indeed, Fierro, he did. And no children. Argentines could see themselves as his children, and he was protective of them. Those whom the Perón couple favored fought for them earnestly."

"Does it surprise you, Sombra? Perón sounds like the leader of a *montonera.* Wasn't he?"

"In many ways he was, Fierro, but he had a vision, too."

"What vision, Sombra?"

"He drew the people out of the saladeros and gave them dignity, making them citizens of a brighter Argentina. He made them feel good and they supported him. He realized it was not enough to just pay them higher salaries; he wanted to add value to their work, so the fruits of their labor would be better paid in larger markets. He promoted industry."

"A hero to me, Sombra. The owners of the saladeros can't have liked him much."

> "Shared history offers the backdrop that both builds expectations and facilitates the communication, while also constraining leadership options. An Argentine leader will have to do a lot of explaining to his followers if he wishes to take a stance different than what Fierro would have done."

"You are right there, Fierro. They hated his guts, as their heirs still do. They fought him, they slandered him, and they cut his access to finance as he sought allies in Chile and Brazil. He had a vision and a strategy, but he was ahead of his time, Fierro. His allies took his money but failed to deliver."

"Traitors, Sombra! Feed the dogs owned by others and you will be left with no food or dogs!"

"Perhaps, Fierro, or perhaps their troubles were larger than Perón's own. It took those countries another four decades to catch up with Perón and unfence their frontiers. By then he had turned into a fiasco."

"What do you mean by that, Sombra? Heroes cannot be fiascos!"

"Well, like most of us, Fierro, Perón did not know how to leave gracefully. He hung on until he was a scarecrow of what he had been."

"If he lasted too long it was because he stopped fighting, Sombra!"

"Yes, though he never became a lap dog, he lasted too long and confused his followers for years to come. There is some wisdom in your fighting after all, Fierro! It is a tough process to sift leaders, but it surely is an effective one!"

"Believe me, Sombra! If a man is no longer capable of holding his own, he ought to either shut up or die with a facón in his belly. That's all."

"Indeed so, Fierro. The issue is whether there is something left in the man by the time he can no longer fight. If he were not totally spent, you would be ushering him away too early, Fierro!"

"Perhaps, but it surely would get rid of the fat assess running saladeros!"

"If they stand to a fight, yes. But most are more cunning than that, Fierro. They make other people fight for them, like lawyers."

"They are not more cunning; they are more cowardly you mean, Sombra!"

"Perhaps, Fierro, but it is a fact you must learn to contend with. As we move north, we will come across many fighting people over many years. Some could have fought with Rosas and Perón, others with the saladero owners. Cowards come in all shapes and sizes, Fierro!"

"So does the Devil, Sombra!" And he crossed himself. "Still, I would have followed Perón!"

"I am sure you would have, Fierro. In a way he followed you, reminding his people that his struggle was very much like yours."

"Did he, Sombra?"

"Indeed he did, Fierro. I will show you how much Perón's style is owed to your own. First look at yourself. Your posture is that of a proud man, bonded with nature. Your attitude is challenging, masculine, rough, susceptible, luxurious and resolute. Your behavior is violent, revengeful, loyal, spiteful, courageous, adventurous, generous and insubordinate, but also friendly. You are also independent, superstitious, clannish. And you inspire respect, fear, nostalgia and support for the underdog.[1]

[1] Adjectives for Martin Fierro were culled from (Bordelois, 1999).

"We were a small country subjected to international capitalism, which suffocated our economy and speculated with the hunger of the Argentine workers. We were a country without direction, and now the direction is our direction, we go where we want to be.

And we allow ourselves to show mankind the way of our justicialismo.

We can say with legitimate pride, that working together, we have built on the old Argentina, unfair, sold-out and betrayed, this new Argentina, fair, free and sovereign."
(Perón, 1947)

Is this how you would like to be seen? Because it is how people will remember you."

"I think it does reflect me, Sombra. At least it shows me as I would like to be seen. What about it?"

"Well, Fierro, you became an icon and your remembered style became a remnant of your times. It even spilled over to the urban environment, as in the urban guapo—all mouth and trousers."

"Do the guapos use *facones*, Sombra?"

"Shorter ones, Fierro, but they do. The flair survives, and communicates. You, Fierro, live in all current Argentine authentic leadership."

"How did this happen, Sombra?"

"Fierro, you became mandatory reading when the current leaders were at school. You are shared history."

"What does it mean, Sombra?"

"This shared history offers the backdrop that both builds expectations and facilitates the communication, while also constraining leadership options. An Argentine leader will have to do a lot of explaining to his followers if he wishes to take a stance different than what you would have done."

"I could tell them what to do, Sombra."

"True, but you would not be there, Fierro. They have to read you to lead them into action, and because they all read you they would all know what you would have done. So much so, that the communicated gaucho style is very effective."

"Sombra, are you suggesting that an Argentine leader would have to behave like I would have done?"

That is precisely it, Fierro! This is why I said that Perón followed you. Because Perón spoke like you would have spoken, his followers understood him immediately and rallied around him."

"I am liking it; tell me more, Sombra!"

"Listen to Perón's 1947 speech. He speaks like you would have, Fierro!"

"I cannot immediately see it, Sombra. He speaks in the language of the cities."

"Of course he does, Fierro, but match his message to your own image. He speaks of pride, that is what your posture stands for. He speaks about rebellion against victimization; you were victimized and your attitude is challenging, masculine, resolute. He links a better future to the dreadful past and speaks of collaboration, and you are clannish as in the *montoneras*. Perón speaks of fairness, and you fight for respect, dignity, and support for the underdog."

"Yes, Sombra, I see it now; there is an almost perfect match between me and Perón's speech."

"What I argue, Fierro, is that larger-than-life Perón would not have elicited the same response from his followers had he not learned to play into the emotional expectations that you aroused seven decades earlier and that found their way into school literature."

> Perón's speech matches the main message of the archetype character Martín Fierro, furthering the possibility of a quicker understanding between the leader and his followers. This is the result of decades of preeminence of the poem *Martín Fierro* in Argentine literature and schooling, but benefits mostly Argentines. Foreigners, or nationals with foreign up-bringing, do not share in the same paradigm with the Argentines, and lack the common understanding with the rest of Argentines, which should render lower efficacy in the communication and in the effectiveness of leadership talent.

"This would mean, Sombra, that in order to be effective, a leader must be able to play into the emotions of his people, and that if he were not familiar with them he would not be as effective?"

"Precisely, Fierro!"

"You are clever, Sombra! This is why only locals could run saladeros effectively!"

"You got it, Fierro! And more, those locals could not be the ones who would imitate the foreign owners of the saladeros, because they would not have a following."

"Sombra, this means that the selection of local leaders of subsidiaries must be turned on its head if it is to be effective!"

"That's it Fierro! We must look at ourselves with our own eyes; we must seek meaning in our own cultural expressions, like yourself."

"Like me, Sombra?"

"Like in your meaning to our people, Fierro! That meaning will help us get organized in ways that suit us best, shaping our organizational behavior."

## Lessons on Fierro's Role in Argentine Leadership

In suggesting that Fierro's message lives on in Argentine leadership, I deconstructed Hernández's poem and a 1947 speech by Juan Domingo Perón, President of Argentina and prominent politician for decades.[2]

I suggested that Perón's speech matches the main message of the archetype character Martín Fierro, furthering the possibility of a quicker understanding between the leader and his followers. This is the result of decades of preeminence of the poem *The Gaucho Martín Fierro* in Argentine literature and schooling, but benefits mostly Argentines.

When not sharing the same paradigm with the Argentines, as would be the case for foreigners or for nationals with foreign upbringing, individuals lack the commonality with the rest of Argentines, which should render lower efficacy in overall communication and in the effectiveness of leadership talent.

I return to this point when discussing Attribution theory of leadership in Chapter 5.

[2] Fragment of Perón's speech "Éramos un pequeño país" (Perón, 1947).

# 4

# The Siege of Montevideo

Language, flags, denominations and distinctions vary along the way north, but the underlying cause for war would remain the same for another century.

The world is changing too fast for the tradition-oriented, earthbound gaucho. Immigrants flock into the cities with modern but strange ideas; political ideas such as government through Republic, or economic ideas such as free trade. Foreigners also enrich themselves faster than the tradition-oriented citizens, expanding their de facto political power. In response to these sweeping changes, Argentine Unitarians, led by Justo José de Urquiza, stand up against Rosas, El Restaurador de las Leyes (The Restorer of Law), and side with the traditionalist Blancos party in Uruguay, led by Oribe, Defensor de las Leyes (Upholder of Laws), and monarchists in Brazil.[1]

Ultimately it was Urquiza, backed by Brazilian monarchists and others, who deposed Rosas and triggered Argentine modernization, including the substantial improvement of the population's education under Sarmiento. The tradition-oriented Brazilians who supported Urquiza never trusted him; their first choice should have been to side with Rosas. But Rosas was too much for them. They knew they would do better with a weaker leader in

[1] Domingo Faustino Sarmiento's assessment of the forces against Rosas sealed the fate of the latter (Sarmiento, 1852, 18; Gil Amate, 2012).

Argentina who would not hamper Brazil's access to Montevideo and Paraguay.

As Fierro and Sombra made progress on their northern destination, they encountered several instances of these ideological clashes with similar protagonists, largely unaware of each other's battles.

On the eastern side of the River Uruguay, Oribe proved to be more of an educationalist than his ally Rosas in Argentina ever was. Oribe had decamped his forces at the Cerrito de la Victoria and built a seventy-five-foot-tall observation tower to peep into the fortressed city of Montevideo, which he would besiege for almost nine years. Oribe could well have been a voyeur. During that time, much to the chagrin of Oribe's gaucho army, there were some battles, though not many, and all were indecisive. Oribe balanced the penchant for immediate results of his gaucho army with the hesitancy of his intellectual supporters. Oribe controlled the land, but Montevideo was a port and it would be supplied by the French and British ships that backed the city.

Fierro and Sombra roamed around the siege, largely unnoticed.

Sombra points out schools and hospitals that Oribe had ordered built. "Now there, Fierro." Sombra signaled, "There is a man who knows what he wants! He knows he is not winning but also knows that if he does win he will need healthy and literate people to run the place, so he takes care of them."

"I see," Fierro sighs, slightly bored.

Sombra continues, "It is not cowardly to sheave the facón and roof the people, feed their stomachs and minds!"[2]

"So that they will become more effective followers at the saladeros, Sombra?"

"Hold it, Fierro!" said Sombra. "We must teach; some will go astray at the saladeros and elsewhere, but others not. Some will

[2] The first and last scene of Akira Kurosawa's film *Throne of Blood,* are particularly relevant to remember here in that they portray the ruins of a fortress and the tombstones of a cemetery while a chorus sings "... lived a proud warrior / Murdered by ambition, / His spirit walking still. / Vain pride, then as now, / Will lead ambition to the kill" (Kurosawa, 1957).

make mistakes, but their mistakes should be smaller than if they knew nothing!"

Fierro was not very interested and changed the subject, "I do not know the ones inside the fortress, but I like these out here, they are like me! I would fight with them. I am sure the ones in the fortress are all Neapolitans, unable to ride a horse!"[3]

"You're probably right, Fierro!" said Sombra. "Among the ones inside, you are likely to find more foreigners. But will they be worse?"

"Fierro, the concept of leader of the crowd, or a pack, will be extremely relevant to understand leadership at saladeros. There we will see the futile attempts of managers at leading people who will fail to evolve into a crowd precisely because the managers of the saladeros will normally lack the catalytic properties referred to by Canetti."

"Yes, they will."

"Why, Fierro?"

"Because they are not like us! I could knife three of them in one blow!"

"No doubt you would, too, Fierro! If they did not blow you first with a cannon!"

"Cowards!" cried Fierro, pulling his knife and brandishing it high in the air against the fortress of Montevideo. "Only cowards would not fight with a facón!"

"Some may be cowards, some not, Fierro," said Sombra. "One thing is for sure, I prefer the respect that goes with courage, accompanied by the assurance that a cannon brings. Why not have both, Fierro? If Oribe had large enough cannons he would have made it into Montevideo already. Like the Turks worked their way into Constantinople! The times of the facón-only battles are coming to a close, Fierro!"

Sombra continued, "Fierro, you mock the Neapolitans inside the fortress of Montevideo, but look at those Carbonari now coming out to fight Oribe's men."

"Who are they, Sombra?"

"They fled Italy for their lives when defeated in a war to liberate Italy from foreign occupation."

[3] For an illustration of Fierro's xenophobia, see section V, "Gringos en la frontera. La estaquiada"; in particular stanza 142 on Neapolitans (Hernández, 2005).

"Why did they come here, Sombra?"

"They went where they would not be caught, ended up in many places."

"What about the ones here, Sombra?"

"These ones landed in Southern Brazil. Pay attention to that one, Giuseppe (Joseph) Garibaldi is his name. He fought in Brazil first and is now fighting here."

"Surprisingly good on horseback for a Neapolitan, Sombra."

"Only on horseback, Fierro? You should have seen him on a small boat fitted with one cannon and putting Brazil's Imperial Navy on the run!"

"Sombra, I see him now picking himself up from the ground where he fell after wounding two of Oribe's men!"

"Fierro, see how he has placed his hat on his sword, straight up, signaling to his men that though he fell he is not dead, so they will continue to fight!"

"Yes, a good montonera leader, Sombra! There he steps over the dead bodies of his comrades to advance and strike!"

> "Garibaldi was a leader of montoneras, in that he was one of those men, Fierro, who precipitate their formation. Montoneras in the Canetti sense of crowds. A crowd is when people become one, blurring the limits between the self and the rest. The achievement of the goal may be directed by a small group of people, rigidly constituted and delimited, of great constancy and perseverance, who may catalyze the formation of the crowd and direct its evolution."

"Good? Only good, Fierro?! This man has fought afoot, on horseback, aboard ships, on three continents—always against absolutism! He was a leader of crowds, Fierro."

"Crowds in what sense, Sombra?"

"In that he was one of those men, Fierro, who precipitate the formation of crowds. Crowds in the Canetti sense of crowds.[4] A crowd is when people become one, blurring the limits between

[4] To Canetti, crowds or "packs"—*montoneras* in Fierro's parlance—have a dynamic of their own, including in their irrational acceptance of the leadership they seek (Canetti, 1962, 85).

the self and the rest.[5] The achievement of the goal may be directed by a small group of people, rigidly constituted and delimited, of great constancy and perseverance, who may catalyze the formation of the crowd and direct its evolution."[6]

"Sombra, do you think Garibaldi was a leader of crowds? Didn't the crowds come later?"

"True, Fierro. Crowds came with the triumph of the secularization of societies.[7] In being uprooted, Garibaldi's comrades were closer to the secular crowd phenomena than to the religious order, which was not on their side."

"You make this sound very important, Sombra, is it?"

"Fierro, the concept of leader of the crowd, or pack, will be extremely relevant to understand leadership at saladeros. There we will see the futile attempts of managers at leading people who fail to evolve into a crowd precisely because the managers lack the catalytic properties referred to by Canetti."

"Fine, I will wait for more; back to this catalyst now. Was Garibaldi a courageous man, Sombra?"

"Indeed he was, Fierro! He saw his friends succumb to the *metraille* of dumb cannons and picked himself up again to fight while wondering why Divine Providence had spared him and not the rest!"

"Always alone, Sombra?"

"Never alone, Fierro. He is an inspiring leader, he has always fought with a core of what you would call Neapolitans, and these may have been the catalysts of the crowd fighting at the Siege of Montevideo. In Brazil, alone after a naval battle against an English

[5] Farfetched as this may have seemed to individualists, recent neurological research into mirror neurons suggests that the human brain comes wired with a port for this network interconnection, and that this may hold an explanation for the working of leadership (Goleman & Boyatsis, 2008, 76).

[6] To Canetti, the crowd is geared for unlimited, all-encompassing growth, where seeking unlimited density, cohesion and equality and is driven toward a shared goal (Canetti, 1962, 32 and 85).

[7] With increasing secularization, religious terminology lost its footing, as suggested by Toynbee arguing that contemporary conversion more readily means converting coal into electricity than turning a soul unto God (Toynbee, 1987, 112).

mercenary, Admiral John Pascoe Greenfell, hired by the Brazilian Imperial Navy, Garibaldi lost many of his closest fighters; he married Anita, a Brazilian, a fireball like himself."[8]

> Hiring teams works best when the individuals are aligned with their leaders. When they are not, it might even backfire. Like it backfired at the French Foreign Legion because same-nationality battalions mutinied against the commanding officer more easily than battalions of varied nationalities.

"Wait! What was an Englishman doing in the Brazilian navy, Sombra?"

"Fierro, it will happen all the time. These countries did not know how to build ships, let alone man them. They fought on the sea with foreign mercenaries."

"Like Garibaldi himself."

"No, Fierro. Garibaldi was not in it for money, neither was the American John Griggs, who led the shipbuilding with which Garibaldi battled at sea in southern Brazil.[9] Garibaldi faced British Admirals John Pascoe Grenfell in Brazil and William Brown in Montevideo."

"Who was this Brown, Sombra?"

"He was another British mercenary, Fierro, this one hired by Rosas. But let us focus on the Garibaldis for now. Together Giuseppe and Anita Garibaldi arrive in Montevideo and offer their services to the city of Montevideo, after buying time as tradespeople. Garibaldi is hired of course, and he brings his battalion of Neapolitans, hence the fireball atop the green mountain on Uruguay's flag, representing the Vesuvius Volcano. Red and green will be their colors."

"Why does he always fight with Neapolitans?"

[8] This book on leadership and management was known in the late nineteenth and early twentieth centuries, when most public leadership was of the masculine variety. Some fascinating characters, such as Anita Garibaldi, wife and combatant with her husband Giuseppe, are best, though regretfully, left on the sidelines. For an account of Anita Garibaldi, see Valerio (2001).

[9] The maritime technology that Oribe's men lacked in Montevideo could have been developed with the help of the foreigners despised by our character Martin Fierro. In southern Brazil, it was precisely two foreigners, an Italian and an American, who build the vessels with which to fight the Brazilian imperial navy, led by another foreigner (Garibaldi & Dumas, 1861, 90–92).

"Good question, Fierro! Montevideo is defended by a legion of Spaniards, another of Frenchmen, and this one of Italians. That, besides Montevideo's own legion plus another of freed slaves. A legion for each crowd. Keep this in mind, Fierro: Our people need to know each well other in order to trust and work and fight together more effectively."

"Well it is obvious, isn't it, Sombra? At the French Foreign Legion they formed battalions by nationality because it was more practical."[10]

"Fierro, hiring teams works best when the individuals are aligned with their leaders.[11] When they are not, it might even backfire. Like it backfired at the French Foreign Legion because same-nationality battalions organize themselves against the commanding officer more easily than battalions of varied nationalities."[12]

"Obvious, Sombra! People who trust each other more than they trust the leader will pack against him when he orders them to do what they would rather not."[13]

The managers of the saladeros will believe in hiring individuals from the market and then will expect them to work well in teams. Instead they should hire montoneras and then ask their leader to collaborate. Montoneras are Canetti's crowds or packs, but it will not be how the saladeros are organized. Their managers will copy the tenets of American Scientific Management, and in applying them to these people, who are not Americans, these tenets will result in lack of engagement and they will forever be lagging in productivity.

[10] The French Foreign Legion was set up largely with veterans of European wars who, unoccupied, had become a nuisance in the streets of France (Windrow & Roffe, 1971, 5).

[11] The Legion's commanding officers were invariably French. The rank and file of the legionnaires were mostly of other nationalities (Duff-Gordon, Lamping & Alby, 1845, 23).

[12] Germans were always overrepresented in the French Foreign Legion, to the point that during World War II, Nazi efforts were directed to infiltrate the Foreign Legion. Consequently, French officers came to believe it would be wiser not to attempt to deploy the Legion in Europe (Windrow & Roffe, 1971, 28).

[13] Indeed, in 1835 the legion preferred to mix the nationalities in the battalions (Boyd, 2008, 123). I owe this insight to Roberto Managau.

"That is perhaps why the saladero leaders hire from the market, Fierro."

"But, Sombra, then they will not get the teamwork they say they are looking for."

"It will be forgotten, Fierro. The managers of the saladeros will hire individuals from the market and then will expect them to work well in teams. Nonsense!"

"Silly, Sombra, they should be hiring montoneras and then ask their leader to collaborate."

"Perhaps they should, Fierro. Montoneras are Canetti's crowds or packs, remember? But it will not be how the saladeros are organized. Their managers will copy the tenets of American Scientific Management, and in applying them to these people, who are not North Americans, those tenets will result in lack of engagement and the saladeros will forever lag in productivity.[14] They will have missed Canetti's teaching, Fierro."

"It doesn't surprise me, Sombra. It is not easy to work with people you do not know well."

"Take Garibaldi as an example, Fierro. He will one day return to Italy, be acclaimed as a hero, and continue to fight, liberating Rome with his Montevideo Tigers, and then head south to take Naples!"

"Why Montevideo Tigers, Sombra?"

"Because from Montevideo he will return to Italy with his Italian friends—some people from Montevideo, close to fifty of them, including Guerilla, a lame dog that sided with him in the battle of Santo Antonio in northwest Uruguay!"

"A lame dog, Sombra?"

[14] Societies oriented toward a clan approach to interpersonal relationships, like most in Latin America see the person as a member of a group, which defines the individual's identity. By hiring from the market people who did not previously know each other, companies are separating them from their webs of relationships. This is why it is hard to create a team out of people who see themselves already as members of and loyal to other teams. Individualist societies, like the one that inspired American Scientific Management, show lower group loyalty and less relational interdependence; in being less constrained by relational attachments, they can fit almost as well nearly everywhere (Fernández, Páez & González, 2005, 35–63).

"Yes, Fierro, such is love. Garibaldi was frequently seen in Italy wearing a white poncho and a horsewhip, which he brought over from Montevideo. Guerilla would always trot between the four legs of Garibaldi's horse."

"What kept them going, Sombra? This was not even their land!"

"In the short term, Fierro? Recognition did. Dispensed generously, even if only through titles only they could be proud of."

"Like what, Sombra?"

"Like those that go with promotions, Fierro. There could well have been more officers than soldiers in Garibaldi's lot. It will be the same in Italy and I dare say throughout this continent. They will have so many officers that many will be performing duties that in regular armies were undertaken by soldiers."

After each battle, Garibaldi would ask around who had done their bit and then recognize them on the spot—an embrace here, a promotion there—no calendar-based assessment periods, no patience with the usual military rules of seniority in career advancement.

"How did promotions happen, Sombra? How would Garibaldi assess their performance in battle?"

"Courage and effectiveness are paramount in that world, Fierro."

"It's obvious to me and it should be to all, Sombra!"

"We agree on that, Fierro. The issue is how effectiveness is to be gauged and how it can be stimulated."

"Well, that is also second nature to me, Sombra; how did Garibaldi deal with that?"

"Fierro, after each battle, Garibaldi would ask around who had done their bit and then recognize them on the spot—an embrace here, a promotion there—no calendar-based assessment periods, no patience with the usual military rules of seniority in career advancement."

"Just like in a montonera, Sombra! Surprising for a Neapolitan."

"Well, Fierro, it is obvious to us, but it will not be as obvious to the owners of the saladeros who not only believe in hiring from the market people who know little of one another, but also ask them to wait for months for an evaluation and eventual recognition!"

> A cause needs at least the perfume of glory to be worthy of a man's life! There is little glory to be promised to a man jerking beef. Pay at a saladero needs to be higher than the pay that would be asked by same men willing to give their lives to a cause. We will see that in Rio de Janeiro where the workers sneak out of the saladeros to moonlight for months at their Samba Schools, for no pay, and still deliver a world-class Carnival parade. During that time they will be something like Canetti's crowd!

"I would walk out if I were working at a saladero, that is if I ever joined one, God forbid!" said Fierro as he crossed himself.

"Saladero owners, geared to meet processes, will prize homogeneity and seek median behavior, Fierro. They will not be good at dealing with true talent, which comes in all shapes and sizes."[15]

"And in the long run, Sombra, what kept them going?"

"A cause, Fierro. Love for a cause. There is no drive more effective than that."[16]

"True, but what did their opponents fight for, Sombra? Was it not a cause, too?"

"Most were waged soldiers, Fierro. Professionals, they like to call themselves, mercenaries to me!"

"Like the workers at the saladeros, Sombra?"

"Cunning you are, Fierro! A cause needs at least the perfume of glory to be worthy of a man's life! There is little glory to be promised to a man jerking beef, so I guess pay at a saladero needs to be higher than the pay that would be asked by the same men willing to give their lives to a cause. We will see that in Rio de Janeiro, where the workers sneak out of the saladeros to moonlight for months at their samba schools, for no pay, and still deliver a world-class Carnival parade, when they will be something like Canetti's crowd!"

[15] Garibaldi's legion was an incongruous assortment of men and children of all ranks. Garibaldi himself could have been taken for an indigenous tribal chief rather than a General (Garibaldi & Dumas, 1861, 270–71).

[16] Upon victory, the commander of Montevideo offered land in the way of compensation to the Italian legion helping defend Montevideo. To that letter the Italians replied: "The Italian officers did not contemplate … when asking for arms and offering their services to the Republic, any other reward but the honor of sharing the perils of the children of the country which had offered them hospitality" (Garibaldi & Dumas, 1861, 199).

"What if, Sombra, the workers were made to believe that salting beef is the path to glory within a cause?"

"Such as, Fierro?"

"Like harvesting sugar cane stalks in Cuba, for example."

"Then they will work like men out of this world, Fierro. But they will need to believe in their leaders, like these believe in Garibaldi. That is only achieved upon proof of generosity and closeness by their leaders."

"Generosity? Give me an example, Sombra!"

"Generosity from simple matters, Fierro, like Garibaldi giving his sole shirt to a comrade who had none, to large ones like sharing the bounty of a take among his soldiers to the point of keeping none for himself."[17]

"Indeed, those examples of generosity are quite something, Sombra."

"Yes, and there is more to it, Fierro."

"Like what, Sombra?"

"Like the issue of distance."

"Distance as in length, Sombra?"

"Emotional distance, Fierro. Northern leadership makes a lot of it, arguing that the best leaders are good at managing the distance that separates them from their followers."[18]

"Managing distances like in being close but not too close, Sombra?"

"Yes, Fierro."

"I would not trust a leader who would not let me know where I stand at all times, Sombra!"

"Precisely, Fierro! That is a difference between us and the Northerners. Some northern authors believe that keeping

> We believe in leaders who act as fathers, sometimes scolding us but always protecting us, always close. Shut us out in the cold and we become orphans. That is at the root of the problem, too many men searching for their father may make us look for a father where we should not.

[17] Generosity is one of the qualities of a Servant Leader (Garibaldi & Dumas, 1861, 229; Ruwhiu & Elkin, 2016, 308–23).

[18] In this managing the distance between leaders and followers, Robert Goffee and Gareth Jones make much of a meeting with Roche pharmaceutical's CEO Franz Humer, when the later seemed to act on stage when answering a question (Goffee & Jones, 2006, 147ff and 194).

people unsure regarding their standing contributes to extracting the most out of them."

"I would not fight for a leader who treated me like that, Sombra; in fact, he would not be a leader at all."

"Well, there you are, Fierro. Latin Americans are different. We believe in leaders who act as fathers, sometimes scolding us but always protecting us, always close. Shut us out in the cold and we become orphans."

"I would not like to feel like an orphan any more than I already am one."

"Indeed, Fierro. I guess that is at the root of the problem, too many men searching for their father may make us look for a father where we should not."

"But Garibaldi was not a manager of emotions; he must have given all out at all times. His people must have loved him, Sombra."

"That love and generosity by Garibaldi is what took people like the Negro Aguyar, a former slave freed in South America, to fight in Italy and ultimately have himself killed in the Siege of Rome."

"Tests like these help sort the men from the rest, Sombra, but without putting the men to test; will the people be able to tell who has courage and who does not?"

> A man who holds his ground will always be respected, but the cannon and the musket have leveled the ground. You no longer have to be born strong to afford to be brave!

"The tests will be different. A man who holds his ground will always be respected, but the cannon and the musket have leveled the ground, Fierro. You no longer have to be born strong to afford to be brave!"

"I hope you are right, Sombra!" cried Fierro. "For I would hate for my children to live in a world of cowards!"

"We all would hate that outcome, Fierro."

"I am not so sure, after what you told me about the saladero, Sombra. It would seem that once deprived of his facón the man has been emasculated."

"Domesticated, perhaps, Fierro. Not emasculated."

"It boils down to the same, Sombra; if the man behaves like a woman, he is a coward!"

"Living in that fortress, Fierro, or working at the saladero, requires accepting rules, yes, but does not take total submission."

"I would draw the line with my facón, Sombra!"

"The law should be enough to draw that line, Fierro."

"The law is interpreted by the judge, Sombra, and he may turn out to be like Vizcacha's judge! My facón would provide me with a good backup!"

"Perhaps you are right, Fierro. There is likely to be a transition until the law works effectively for all, freeing righteous men from fear."

"With a facón I fear no one, Sombra."

"Even if he had a gun, Fierro?"

"In that case I would have to choose the time for my attack, Sombra, but retreating is not cowardice when it is to avoid the worst!"

"Now you are beginning to sound wise, Fierro. Just like José Artigas said!"

"Yes, I would have followed Artigas, Sombra. He was a hero to the Uruguayans, and many in the Argentine Mesopotamia. Artigas would not have run a saladero!"

"Only God knows what Artigas would have done in a saladero, but it is likely that under Artigas, the saladero would not have acted like the slimy ones that Professor Gore depicts."[19]

"How can we hit the right balance, Sombra?"

"Through education, Fierro. Canetti argued that it was imperative to control the survivor instinct of the saladero owners and that the key to that was to humanize command."[20]

"I am not sure that is the only way, Sombra. To me, educated people tend to behave like cowards."

"If so, we would need better education, Fierro; for our true enemy is not the foreman at the saladero, not even the owner of the saladero. Our enemy is disease! Fire is the enemy, Fierro! Storms are our enemies!"

[19] These were the ones who pretended they were working, but really were making sure that they could not be blamed or criticized later for something going wrong (Gore, 2009).

[20] Lack of humanity in leadership gives place to all sorts of evils (Murdoch & Conradi, 1997, 191).

"It is not enough, Sombra!"

"I'll tell you what, Fierro, around Oribe's port, at Buceo, a man will live who could have run an army of true men but chose to become a doctor to heal people. Gustavo Prunell will be his name. You will respect him when the time comes to meet him; you will look each other in the eye and you will recognize each other. I am sure you will."

"So what, Sombra?"

"You will have recognized a leader, Fierro, like yourself, but without a facón. He chose to have a family and do well by his wife, his children, and those who meet him."

"Wine also heals, Sombra!"

"Indeed it helps, Fierro, and close to Prunell as well you will find Javier Carrau who built a superb wine business out of a vineyard!

If we can build an organization that allows choices like those of Prunell and Carrau to be made and stick, we will have succeeded."

"Will it be possible without war, Sombra?"

"Some war will be necessary, Fierro. To cover your ass in it you will need people who are not protagonists but who are loyal to death, like Philippe Sauval."

"Another Neapolitan, Sombra?"

"Only if you went back to Bourbon times, Fierro! Sauval is as criollo as mate and as loyal as a dog."

"Speaking of Sauval, I had my Cruz, did you know Fierro?"[21]

"Yes, I know. He covered your ass."

"He was my Sauval, Sombra!"

We will need all—fighters, healers and guardians—to fight and build simultaneously.

Oribe is on the right track, Fierro, even though he will lose. Now let us call it a day. The horses are tired and so are we."

"Talking of horses, Sombra, why is yours called Turena?"

[21] Dispatched to hunt Fierro, Sargeant Cruz, in seeing the bravery and independence with which Fierro fought back, Cruz changed sides and joined Fierro, which is also another name for the sword, as Cruz in Spanish stands for Cross. The names Fierro and Cruz, sword and cross, recall the Moor-fighting Spanish Catholic propensity for the dramatic and heroic, and their punctilious sense of honor.

"It used to be Felipe Ángeles's horse, Fierro."

"Ángeles, did you say? The Mexican general who used to name his horses with the names of French generals?"

"The same one, Fierro; and in being a supporter of Pancho Villa, he was not friendly to your father."

"So I heard. We will no doubt learn more about them when we get closer."

"No doubt we will, Fierro. What about your horse, Fierro?"

"Spinoza is his name, Sombra."

"Like the Spanish-Dutch Jewish philosopher?"

"The same. He was at odds with all shades of Christians besides Jews and still believed we are all one with Nature. Like me and my horse; one, Sombra," and he spurred his horse which neighs, "*Nam nihil in natura datur, quod jure posset dici hujus esse, et non alterius; sed omnia omnium sunt.*"[22]

## Lessons from the Siege of Montevideo

Gauchos are always on the move. But Oribe was stuck in Cerrito de la Victoria for almost nine years. Holding gauchos in one place for a couple weeks must have been difficult enough. After a time, they are not gauchos anymore, and what is left of them may not be good enough to fight. Oribe's educated staff delayed action; his army grew old and eventually left without taking Montevideo.

Oribe's siege of Montevideo defeated his organization. His ragtime army was pinned down with little function, his men idle and—lacking in challenges—unable to be evaluated or sorted out for promotions, which were lacking in any case. Sarmiento had perceived the same in Rosas's ragtime army. It is hard to understand, organizationally, what kept these men at the Cerrito de la Victoria for so long. It cannot have been the goal, for that became increasingly elusive and finally naught. It is quite likely that it was not the same men we are talking about, in the sense that some must have returned to their origins, further even than the Argentine Mesopotamia. Some may have

[22] "For Nature offers nothing that can be called this man rather than another, under nature everything belongs to all" (Spinoza, 1667, chapter 2, paragraph 23). Translated by A. H. Gossett (1883).

joined the Cerrito forces later. Some foreigners may have abandoned their families elsewhere and started new ones closer to the Cerrito. Even those who stayed for the whole eight years ceased to be gauchos.

"Sombra, what did we learn here?"

"Quite a few important things to look out for in our next chapters, Fierro."

"Like what?"

"Fierro, there are important lessons on alliances and strategy, on leadership styles, on performance evaluation and promotions, on incentives, and on teamwork."

"On all that, Sombra?"

"Perhaps not equally on all, but let us review the elements of this Siege of Montevideo."

"In the first place, Fierro, why would Oribe have the support of Rosas against the city of Montevideo?"

"That's easy, Sombra! For the same reasons I would have sided with them! They hold the same values and stand against the same enemy: Foreign encroachment on our land! I hate those Neapolitans and the boats they arrive on."

"But some of our ancestors arrived the same way, Fierro! Rosas and Oribe are not fighting for values any differently than the natives did at the time of the conquest. Rosas and Oribe are only trying to hold on to an income flow that is challenged by more recent immigrants."

> When the drama is removed from a task, like it frequently is at a saladero, small feats will soon be forgotten. Annual assessments will mostly reflect the last few weeks' performance, particularly among people with a strong present orientation. Performance evaluations will fail to provide a fair assessment of performance.

"So be it, Sombra."

"But you are missing the point, Fierro. Brazilians were monarchists; in being tradition-oriented they should have sided with Rosas, not with the immigrants defending Montevideo, which tended to the Republican side."

"I do not think the Brazilians sided with Urquiza against Rosas, Sombra. I think they just wanted to weaken Rosas; once they had him out, they would pounce on Montevideo later."

"You may be right, Fierro. That should have added resolve to Oribe to make a go at Montevideo the sooner the better."

"He failed, in assessing his natural allies, then?"

"I think he did, Fierro. Rather than waiting out a city that was being supported by the sea, he should have competed. Why not compete, Fierro?"

"I do it all the time, Sombra, facón in hand!"

"I did not mean duel, Fierro, but work, team up with the new competencies arriving on those boats and do better together!"

"Those Neapolitans are different from us, Sombra. Too different."

"Not more different than the imperial Portuguese that will side with Urquiza to demote Rosas and cut Oribe's lifeline, Sombra."

"True, Sombra. Oribe encircled himself; over eight years, too!"

"He never managed to cut off the supplies that Montevideo received by sea either, Sombra! Why did he fail at that?"

"We are not fish, Sombra! We ride horses on land!"

"Precisely. Did you not wonder why Rosas resorted to Captain Brown to lead his navy against Captain Garibaldi?"

"What? Garibaldi led Montevideo's navy as well?"

"He did, Fierro. Neither Montevideo nor Rosas had seafaring fighters."

"Good point, Sombra. The almost nine years Oribe hung around Montevideo would have been enough to build or secure a few armed boats."

"Precisely, Fierro. Oribe failed at filling the competencies gap that finally did him in. He was stuck on a horse. Garibaldi had built gunboats in Southern Brazil, before he arrived in Montevideo."

"Would this lack of seafaring competencies be carried over into the future, Sombra?"

"Indeed they will, Fierro. More than a century later these countries will still depend on foreign ships to get their produce

"Workers work best in teams when they know each other. Recruiting should take this into account, by recruiting through loyalty webs, which are mostly geographically based. Recruiting for a saladero may be more effective if you leave it up to the workers to tell you who they would like to work with."

to their markets. Path dependency is a curse, not a course, Fierro!"[23]

"And on leadership, Sombra, what is there to learn from the siege?"

"Well, if the inability to assess the match the competencies needed with those available, and to do something about the gap, were not enough to write off a leader, we should turn to Garibaldi for inspirations, should we not?"

"True, Sombra, I got to like that Neapolitan!"

"First of all, Garibaldi was moved by a cause: To fight absolutism wherever it may be. He had convictions, without which it is hard to persuade anyone. He also had a track record, which helped people decide to risk their lives for him; he was generous and he led from the front, putting his own life at risk when he asked his people to put their own lives at stake."

"Yes, Sombra, he had the true leader's authenticity."

"Precisely, Fierro. He had the qualities that enticed people who would coalesce around him."

"And form the Canetti crowds, Sombra? Like the leaders of the montoneras?"

"Like them, but with a more humanized style of leadership, Fierro. Garibaldi was not here to sow destruction. Much to the contrary. Still, Fierro, Garibaldi was more effective leading his own, wasn't he?"

"Yes, those Neapolitans!"

[23] Men locked into their cattle-slaughtering past at saladeros would be unlikely to take to the sea. Path dependency links the present to the past, as in "history matters." It presumes that the energies that drive toward the future come from the past, with insufficient input from the "hopes, fears or expectations" that may also create the future (Tamás, 2011, 95).

"Precisely, Sombra, the Neapolitans. But Montevideo's defense was organized in legions based on nationality, was it not?"

"Yes, Fierro, so what; it is so obviously necessary, is it not?"

"Well, Sombra, there is a hint of a requirement for organizational effectiveness there, isn't there?"

"Yes, but besides the obvious fact that people need to speak the same language to communicate effectively, what else do you make out of it?"

"Fierro, it might not be only language, but familiarity, loyalty webs, mutual dependence bred and ratified by past behavior; those help make a pack, or a Canetti crowd."

"True, Sombra, those would be harder to see, or hear."

"Indeed, Fierro, because organizing fighters by nationality is so obvious we may fail to see the significance it entails: Workers work best in teams when they know each other. Recruiting should take this into account, by recruiting through loyalty webs, which are mostly geographically based."

"Aha! Sombra, you mean that recruiting for a saladero may be more effective if you leave it up to the workers to tell you who they would like to work with?"

"I think so, Fierro; it is still only a hunch. But we will see how it works out in other chapters."

"But Sombra, if they were all friends, how would you assess performance?"

"Like Garibaldi did, by results. After each battle he would ask around who did well that day."

"That is more obvious in a war context than in saladeros, is it not, Sombra?"

"More dramatic perhaps, Fierro. But work at any saladero is not as routine as you would have it. Any task offers plenty of occasions to assess performance, because there are many ways to skin cattle."

"What's the trick then, Sombra?"

"To assess performance frequently, Fierro. If the drama is removed from a task, like it frequently is at a saladero, small feats will soon be forgotten. Annual assessments will mostly reflect the last few weeks' performance, particularly among people with a strong present orientation."

Once basic needs are considered, outstanding performance can be rewarded by recognition by an authentic leader, one that like Garibaldi is not in it just for himself. Not easy to find, this is why we have saints, they provide the true benchmark.

"And this would contribute to kill motivation to work, Sombra?"

"If not to kill, to substantially undermine it, Fierro."

"And how would you reward outstanding performance, Sombra?"

"Once basic needs are considered, Fierro? Through recognition by an authentic leader, one that, like Garibaldi, is not just in it just for himself. Not easy to find, this is why we have saints, they provide the true benchmark."

# 5

# Fierro and Sombra Discuss Leadership Theory

> "To build, to make, to create, one needs teams. Teams blend traits; some follow, some lead. It depends on the circumstances and the tasks to be accomplished. What we need to understand is how best to select the right people to lead the followers for the benefit of all."

Fierro and Sombra woke up the next morning as hides and jerked beef were being embarked for export at Oribe's Puerto del Buceo. They chatted idly by a campfire. Not bound by the "time is money" aphorisms that rule the North, they may head for Brazil today or tomorrow, it makes no difference to them, not least because they are both dead. But they chatted still, and after the Siege of Montevideo, the subject of leadership is as good as any other to test each other on the subject of Leadership.

"There goes meat from a saladero to feed the slaves of Brazil and Cuba!" cried Fierro. "Food for slaves made by emasculated men! What a world, Sombra!"

"Fierro, forget the saladeros, let me tell you the story of the Saraiva Brothers, true heroes on horseback. Today we are heading northeast, toward their land and into Brazil."

"Go on, Sombra, but waste no time with lawyers and generals; give me men, raw men!"

"Let me tell you something about raw men, Fierro. Raw men, by whom you are likely to mean courageous men, may not be that useful."

"Can one do without them, Sombra?"

"No, but one cannot do only with them, for they are likely to come with other traits, like disobedience."

"So what, Sombra? You want obedient men to lead? Be a shepherd then, Sombra, and lead sheep!"

"Fierro, you are confounding me! To build, to make, to create, one needs teams. Teams blend traits; some follow, some lead. It depends on the circumstances and the tasks to be accomplished. What we need to understand is how best to select the right people to lead the followers for the benefit of all."

"Sombra, it is not that difficult. Just let the people choose the leader!"

"Perhaps you are right, Fierro. Perhaps I have been confounded by reading too much management theory."

"Leadership theory sounds rather fascistic to me, Sombra! Drop it!"

"Perhaps you are right, Fierro, this is why early leadership theory, about a century after Oribe, focused on traits of leaders.[1] This approach was easy because intuitively it seemed correct, but did not tell us much more than we already knew."

"Of course, Sombra! One only needs to look a person in the eyes to tell if one would want to follow him or not! It is a very intimate decision."[2]

"True, Fierro. But that is a sensation that cannot be readily exchanged with others."

"Bullshit, Sombra! Every gaucho in a montonera knows who the leader is! Nobody in Salta doubted Güemes, Aráoz in Tucumán, or Quiroga in the Llanos!"[3]

"But there you are! There are several montoneras, and several leaders. Why follow one and not the other? That is the question, Fierro!"

"OK, go on, Sombra."

[1] Bird (1940); Stogdill (1948); Mann (1959).

[2] Behrens (2010).

[3] Sarmiento (2000).

"Then, during the 1930s and 1940s, studies on behavior enabled people to focus on how leaders went about their work and how they did it.[4] We were told that the style of leadership was important as well. There was one type of behavior oriented toward productivity and another toward relationships. That was a step forward because it brought tasks and relationships to the stage and it promoted self-awareness, too."

Management theory is a Northern thing. So is business leadership theory. Leadership theory deals with the relationship between leaders and followers. Followers have been mostly a nuisance because they are too many. Thus they were conveniently put aside and focus was bestowed upon the leaders, who are fewer and more charming to deal with.

"It makes sense, Sombra. It is getting better. Tell me more!"

"Yes, Fierro, these thinkers were not obtuse; they were simply groping for an explanation of a very difficult issue. Of course, a stage requires a particular time and space. By the 1950s and 1960s, leadership became situational, which was practical and good because it called for an adaptive leadership style that brought the followers into the picture; this is how the focus fell on delegating, supporting, and directing according to the circumstances."[5]

"Yes, I can see that, Sombra. Just like in a montonera!"

"Once the followers were brought on stage, Fierro, we were bound to admit they have expectations to be met, and we got the Contingency theory, where the outcome is the result of a parallelogram of forces and structure: The relation between leaders and led, the amount of structure, and the issue of power, all determine a style and effectiveness of leadership.[6] This is how we learned that task-oriented leaders are best at handling routine or crises, while relationship-oriented ones are better in less stressful situations."

Leadership theory made a wide turn. Once we get back to charisma we are very close to admitting that followers attribute to leaders' qualities what they find acceptable.

[4] Lewin and Lippitt (1938); Lewin, Lippitt and White (1939).
[5] Howells and Becker (1962); Leavitt (1951); Shartle (1951).
[6] Fiedler (1978); Vroom and Jago (1998); Yukl (1998).

"Perhaps Oribe was relationship oriented, Sombra? Otherwise, how could he hold so many men at one place for so long? Certainly, task oriented he was not! He did nothing but wait!"

"Not so simple, Fierro! In the first place, Oribe had fought many battles, well into Argentina, as far as Jujuy. He could handle a task well. There must have been two Oribes, one capable of fighting, another capable of waiting. The circumstances changed, perhaps Oribe did, too."

"I do not think that it is so easy, unless Oribe had gotten old, Sombra. Perhaps there was a lack of alternative leaders."

"It could well be, Fierro. But once you admit followers have a say in the leader's effectiveness, you are bound to go further along this line, and that is how we got Path-Goal theory: In order to enhance performance, the leader must be flexible enough to match the workers' motivation."[7]

"Gauchos are not workers, Sombra!"

"True, Fierro, but think of the saladeros."

"Those are not men, Sombra!"

"Fierro, be sensible! The workers at the saladeros are men with wives and children to upkeep. What motivates them to work?"

"Pay does, Sombra! Pay! That's all!"

"Pay may motivate them to play at working, but not to give their all to it. You fought in montoneras, Fierro. Was there pay involved in your offering your life to it?"

"No, it was fun! And what fun it was, Sombra! The call of danger was hard to resist."[8]

"It was deadly, too. Remember, Fierro?"

"Yes, and I lost many friends, Sombra. But it was not pay. Yes, there was a bounty, but even if there had been none, we would have gone along for the thrill of it!"

"You talk about friends at work, Fierro, and bounty. How was the bounty distributed?"

"Why? Each took what they needed, Sombra."

"Did some take more, Fierro?"

"Some did, I did not like those as much."

"What did you do when you did not like it, Fierro?"

[7] House (1971); Bass, Avolio and Atwater (1996); Sashkin (2004).

[8] As with Hemingway's fascination with danger and death in MacLeish (1961).

"Sometimes I left and joined another montonera. I see your point, Sombra."

"Precisely, Fierro. Once we put the followers center stage, we learn that they have relationships, too; and that, with regards to the leader, there are 'in groups' and 'out groups,' and that decisions will be weighed differently by members of both groups. This brings us to the Leader-Member Exchange (LMX) theory, where the role of effective communication becomes crucial.[9] Once the leaders are brought down on a par with their subordinates, they will be asked to endorse explicit values, ethics and goals—both long and short term."

"I see, Sombra; it is up to the leader to ensure that pay is fairly distributed if he expects people to remain with him, because there are always other montoneras."

"But pay, you said yourself, Fierro, is not that important."

"True, it is not."

"So what kept you in the montonera when the outcome was unfair?"

"The leader did, Sombra, the leader was enough. Facundo Quiroga was great, he was mesmerizing!"[10]

"Precisely, Fierro. This is why the leader-follower relationship was humanized, giving place to Transformational Leadership, which—in seeking to inspire—allows for the role of charisma, too, with the ensuing emphasis on sharing in the leader's "vision."[11] Still, there are the hardliners who will stress the role of compensation for efforts, which is the Transactional Leadership Theory, which runs in the background, so to speak. For you need to distribute fairly the bounty, or pay, to hold the organization together."

"I do not think it is as much about pay as about protection, Sombra."

When a gaucho enters a montonera to follow a leader, the leader is the most powerful and the gaucho will do all that is necessary for the montonera to succeed. But the gaucho expects in return that the leader be there for him, no matter what.

[9] Cogliser and Schriesheim (2000).

[10] Chasteen (1995, 6).

[11] Conger and Kanugo (1998); Sashkin (1988; 2004).

"Are you referring to Transactional Leadership Theory, Fierro?"

"Yes, Sombra, there is an exchange between the leader and the follower, yet it is not about money, but about allegiance, loyalty."

"That is an interesting concept, Fierro. You suggest that the montoneras are held together by an implicit contract in which loyalty is exchanged for protection?"

"Yes, Sombra. That is what I think."

"You may be right, Fierro, and that may well be the crux of the power of the paternalist leader in populist regimes, like Perón in Argentina, Vargas and Lula in Brazil, Castro in Cuba, or Chavez in Venezuela."

> "We have to work out a leadership theory ourselves, because the available leadership theory was developed mostly by foreigners who never really experienced the tension of being led by people who are moved by different reasons."

"Yes, there is an exchange, Sombra, only that it is not a mercenary one."

"In what sense, Fierro?"

"The exchange must be perceived to be unbounded."

"What do you mean now, Fierro?"

"Neither allegiance nor protection may have limits. It is an all-or-nothing exchange."

"You are right; loyalty cannot be divided nor can care be measured. Very Medieval, Fierro, and it is not what Northern Hemisphere professors tell us. They argue that followers, like the gauchos in a montonera, accept a degree of ambiguity and uncertainty from the leader."[12]

"I do not know about northern montoneras, Sombra. But there can be no uncertainty in the commitment between a montonera leader and his gauchos. Should the leader fail to deliver, he must at least be seen to be trying his best. That is not uncertainty but impotence in the face of more powerful demons, which is regrettable, but acceptable."

[12] Goffee and Jones (2006).

"Indeed, very Medieval, Fierro!"

"Call it what you wish, Sombra, that is what it is like."

"So, back to saladeros."

"Those are not montoneras, Sombra!"

"But they could be organized into montoneras that jerk beef, could they not?"

"Hard to fathom, but continue, Sombra."

"Let us imagine a saladero in which the montonera leader is boss, Fierro."

"That is not so hard to imagine."

"And the rest of the gauchos toil at jerking beef because they are convinced that, say, that food will feed a friendly army fighting for them."

> Northern foreigners have more trouble with emotional outbursts than we do. They tend to be more controlled and to have difficulties with emotional outbursts. Outbursts send a clear message; they convey how strongly one believes in something. Our emotions will need to be explained, then they will forget, because these saladero kings are rotated. They spend a few years here and when they are about to learn they are sent elsewhere and have to learn all over again.

"Yes, so what, Sombra?"

"Imagine, Fierro, that the army cannot pay for the jerked beef and the gauchos are made to go unpaid. The montonera leader must be seen to have been caught in a tight spot and will need to request the gauchos' support."

"Will he get it, Sombra?"

"If they are convinced that he deserves that support, yes, Fierro."

"So they must believe. If they were lied to, the boss might pay for it with his own life. The facón draws the line. The trouble only appears when honor has been lost, Sombra. What about Oribe?"

"What about him, Fierro?"

"Because there was no fighting, there was no fun, Sombra. He must have paid the gauchos something, but did Oribe have a vision?"

"He must have had one, Fierro. After all, he was educating his lot. What would he educate them for if he had no vision of tomorrow? He also had a judiciary and a parliamentary body that issued

When Darwin got off the *Beagle* he bumped into some gauchos whom he perceived as graceful as well as untrustworthy: "whilst making their exceedingly graceful bow, they seem quite as ready, if occasion offered, to cut our throat." If that was the British perception of the gauchos it is understandable that the owners of the saladeros would entrust the running of the saladeros to those who looked more like themselves than the gauchos.

laws and regulations. There was the embryo of a country in that organization; yes, he must have had a vision that appealed to his followers."

"And what about the saladeros, Sombra?"

"Well, that is a different organization isn't it, Fierro? Put it this way, if there were other saladeros, the unsatisfied workers would vote with their feet by moving to another saladero. If there were only one saladero and pay was unsatisfactory, but the leader had charisma, they would stay."

"Sheep!" cried Fierro.

"What else could they do?"

"Take over the saladero, Sombra! It's obvious!"

"What if the jerked beef importer in Brazil were also the owner of the saladero, Fierro? When taking over the saladero, which is the easy part, would you not end up with a saladero with no clients?"

"So what? We would have to learn to eat jerked beef! That's less of an affront than working for nothing, Sombra!"

"It is never for nothing, Fierro. They get the balance just right. They pay enough to keep the people quiet at work. There is another issue at play."

"Something worse?"

"I am not sure it is worse, Fierro, but if the owner of the saladero is a foreigner, how can we ensure the match between the leader and the followers?"

"True, it is impossible, Sombra!"

"I wouldn't say impossible, Fierro; but difficult, yes!"

"What does your theory say, Sombra?"

"It doesn't."

"The theory is a Neapolitan thing, isn't it, Sombra?"

"I wish it were, because as we will soon all be Neapolitans here, the issue would be easier to solve. It gets much worse!

Latin Americans are group oriented; among us, charisma is more important than among those in the north.[13] The people who run the saladeros can be quite different from us, and hence manage us poorly, too."

"Why did this happen, Sombra? Would not a facón in their bellies be enough feedback?"

"It would, and it has been tried, Fierro."

"So?"

"Well, once you put a facón into the belly of one, the word spreads and foreigners stop investing here and buying from us, Fierro."

"So?"

"Nobody lasted enough to tell, Fierro. Not even Perón! It is not the way. Proper feedback, as opposed to the 'facón in the belly' reaction, is essential in organizational practice because perceptions count in implicit relationship frameworks, as in LMX; leaders would want to know how followers attribute ratings to them.[14] Besides, followers' characteristics may moderate the effectiveness of Transformational Leadership, the approach that inspires higher achievements, and therefore shapes performance, or may even influence the leader's behavior. Lying can also occur, seeking to inspire without really meaning to."[15]

"Of course, Sombra, even Facundo Quiroga could not do all he wanted. But he did not need to ask for feedback. He knew. He could tell."

"OK, Quiroga did not lie, perhaps. But it is harder for foreigners 'to know,' Fierro. Besides, not all followers are alike, which makes it far worse for the foreign leader. This is why delving into the issue of followers' personalities and their perception of Transformational Leadership is likely to open a new avenue of research; because, if follower response is allowed to vary according to personality,[16] one must also assume that it may vary according to culture as well."

[13] Pillai and Meindl (1998).

[14] Uhl-Bien (2003); Uhl-Bien, Graen and Scandura (2000).

[15] Bass and Steidlmeier (1999).

[16] Hetland, Sandal and Backer Johnsen (2008). Schyns and Sanders (2007).

"What does culture have to do with it, Sombra? We are all alike, aren't we?"

"Well, not really; 'they' have more trouble with emotional outbursts than we do, Fierro."

"Do they? Why?"

"They are more controlled, Fierro."

"But an emotional outburst can not only send the message straight, it also conveys how strongly you believe in something!"

"Precisely, Fierro. But it might not be perceived as such by everyone; it will need to be explained.[17] Then they will forget, because these saladero kings are rotated. They spend a few years here and—when they are about to learn—they then are sent elsewhere and have to learn all over again."[18]

"What a waste, Sombra!"

> Attribution theory becomes central to leadership theory because it makes followers' perceptions of leaders fundamental to leadership qualities.

"Indeed, Fierro. At least one Norwegian study has already shown that there was no correlation to be found between the leader's personality and Transformational leadership.[19] This suggests that there seems to be evidence of this, at least between some Europeans, North Americans and Middle Easterners,[20] even if one were to choose to neglect the route taken by GLOBE (Global Leadership and Organizational Behavior Effectiveness research program), which rendered charisma a paramount attribute of leaders across the world."[21]

"So, charisma is all! Sombra! I knew it all along!"

[17] As Antonakis did: "Emotional outbursts can be useful, symbolic, and engender follower identification and trust, as long as these emotions reflect collective sentiments and moral aspirations." In Why emotional intelligence does not predict leadership effectiveness: A comment on Prati, Douglas, Ferres, Ammeter and Buckley" (2003, 359).

[18] Uhl-Bien, Marion and McKelvey (2007).

[19] Hetland and Sandal (2003), particularly p. 164.

[20] Schyns, Felfe and Blank (2007), in particular p. 510 and following.

[21] House et al. (2004).

"Yes, it is almost all, because charisma here is different here from charisma there!"

"So, put one of us to run the saladeros!"

"It is not a bad idea at all, Fierro. The trouble is that the choice is not made by us but by them."

"Who, the Neapolitans?"

"Worse, Fierro, much worse!"

"What can be worse, Sombra? Is it that they choose among our people the ones who look like them?"

"Precisely, Fierro. Who else would the foreigners side with? Remember Darwin, when he got off the *Beagle* he bumped into some gauchos whom he perceived as both graceful and untrustworthy: "Whilst making their exceedingly graceful bow, they seem quite as ready, if occasion offered, to cut our throat."[22] If that was the British perception of the gauchos, it is understandable that the owners of the saladeros would entrust the running of the saladeros to those who looked more like themselves, than the gauchos."

Effective leaders will want to become effective managers of the emotions of their followers. One way of achieving this management will be through evoking follower emotions, such as perceptions of sincerity and intention, through emotional displays. This conceptualizes leadership as an emotional process where leaders display and evoke emotions.

"But that does not excuse foreigners from siding with traitors! Sombra! Are you quivering when it is time for all-out war?"

"I would not call them traitors, Fierro; they are just people like us who ingratiate themselves better with the owners of the saladeros."[23]

"Not traitors, transvestites then?"

"Closer, Fierro, closer."

[22] Darwin (1948).

[23] Peoples of different cultures may root for different characters, like in the Coyote and the Roadrunner cartoons; as in Behrens (2009).

"Which is the way forward, Sombra? What do the books tell you?"

"Very little, Fierro. The books were written by them."

"The owners of the saladeros? Their foremen?"

"Worse, the leadership books were written by their professors, Fierro!"

"Then we must write our own books, Sombra!"

"We are at it right now!"

"Which is the way forward then, Sombra?"

"Fierro, attribution theory becomes central to leadership theory because it makes followers' perceptions of leaders fundamental to leadership qualities.[24] This is what you tell me about Facundo Quiroga."

"Yes, yes. Continue, Sombra!"

"This is why effective leaders will want to become effective managers of the emotions of their followers.[25] One way of achieving this management will be through evoking followers' emotions, such as perceptions of sincerity and intention, through emotional displays.[26] This conceptualizes leadership as an emotional process through which leaders display and evoke emotions.[27] This is why Perón was so effective when communicating with Argentines. He was speaking to people brought up reading you!"

"It is all about emotions, Sombra! You are beginning to get it! It is not difficult among gauchos in a montonera, Sombra. We've been there!"[28]

"Precisely, Fierro. But there are different montoneras with different leaders. We must learn from them all what they have in common in order to guide the management of the saladeros."

"That shouldn't be difficult, Sombra."

[24] Martinko and Thomson (1998).

[25] Humphrey (2002).

[26] Pescosolido (2002).

[27] Dasborough and Ashkanasy (2003).

[28] While it might not all be about emotions, there is no question that attention to emotions are creeping into the charismatic leadership theory, as shown by Tal and Avishag (2015).

The less information people have about others, the more they project their views over the unknown. Therefore, under current educational and communication frameworks from around the world, particularly those that dominate in southern and eastern countries, we ought to consider the northern business leader as relatively unknown, thus weakening his/her possibility as a global business leader.

"You would be surprised, Fierro. There are montoneras of professors as well, and they defend their turf as you would yours! Yet, difficult as it may be to make a falsifiable science out of impressions, it is worth trying, for then we will be in a better position to make more of the Wharton/GLOBE proposition that charisma universally rules in leadership. In the absence of that explanation, knowing that all cultures require charisma of a leader is not the same as knowing what each culture perceives as charisma. Behrens pointed out that charisma may be perceived differently by Brazilians with regard to foreigners, in the sense that Brazilians prefer to be led by Brazilians."[29]

"Of course, Sombra! I certainly do not want to be bossed around by a Neapolitan! First they will have to learn to ride horseback!"

"Move on, Fierro. We will soon all be Neapolitans!"

"Whatever! Give me a gaucho leader!"

"Precisely, Fierro."

"Well, then, go ahead, Sombra! Gallop for it!"

[29] Behrens (2010).

# 6

# Fierro and Sombra Follow the Federalist Revolt in Southern Brazil

"Fierro, you and I know that heroes on horseback were always more frequent in the Southern Pampas, one land with fluid boundaries encompassing Argentina, Uruguay and Southern Brazil, where people do not feel bounded by fancy international treaties."

"Just as well, Sombra!"

"Perhaps, Fierro, and because the land and the people were one, poor economic policies on one side of the frontier would show on the other. People on both sides suffered equally."

"Nowhere else to go?"

"Indeed, Fierro. This may be a bonus, because when people cannot run away from their problems they are forced to face them."

"Now, Sombra, moving on is not running away."

"Perhaps not, Fierro, but it amounts to the same. In any case, Southern Brazilian gauchos would not easily understand how famine could prevail among so many cattle."

"Nor do I, Sombra! True gauchos would kill the cattle and eat it."

"Well, they did, Fierro, but it was not their cattle; and with fewer cattle around, the saladeros could not meet the sales terms they had agreed to."

"To hell with the saladeros, Sombra! Which side are you on?"

"The side doesn't matter, Fierro, at least not as much as the outcome, which is obvious to anyone who cares, as you do. There will be war and we are heading there. The Americans in San Francisco know it because Ambrose Bierce has telegraphed his paper; besides, he published an article in Buenos Aires's *La Prensa.* When the Brazilian Republican Julio de Castilhos wins elections for Governor in Brazil's southernmost state, Rio Grande do Sul, a revolution will start. One country could be made out of Uruguay and Rio Grande do Sul. It will not happen, but they will try."[1]

"I am liking it, Sombra; it was rather boring at the Cerrito de la Victoria."

"Yes, the action is here, on the frontier, Fierro. The situation is so tense one can feel it in the air."

"Tell me more, Sombra, what is coming?"

"Gumercindo and Aparício Saraiva were brothers, Fierro.[2] Gumercindo being the eldest."

"What were they, Sombra?"

"Landowners, but gauchos nonetheless."

"Like your Fabio?"

"More like your own children, Fierro. Rougher than Fabio, but with land. They were frontiersmen, Fierro. Both spoke Spanish and Portuguese as well, or as badly, as it is humorously mentioned. Gumercindo lived this first thirty years in Uruguay, but persecutions led him to cross the border."

"I know the feeling, Sombra," Fierro said, while spurring Spinoza.

"I know you do, Fierro; it is the same all over. Gumercindo was rugged in outdoor skills and could jump on a bareback mustang in a stride. Besides, he had moved cattle from one place to another for years; he knew the fields like few do."

"He sounds like me, Sombra."

"You could have been Gumercindo, Fierro. Except that Gumercindo had already established himself. He had a *patrón* who was a former Monarchist Brazilian, Silveira Martíns. This man launched a revolution against Republican Castilhos and dragged Gumercindo into it."[3]

[1] Friede (2015).

[2] The brothers were known as Saraiva in Brazil and as Saravia in Uruguay. There are quite a few images of Gumercindo and his men: https://goo.gl/UtFBN2. Accessed January 26, 2017.

[3] Gumercindo's troops were referred to as "Maragatos," which is the name attributed to the Spanish born in Maragataria, in the province of León, Spain; once more suggesting that, as in the Siege of Montevideo, people make teams with those that they already know.

"They fought in montoneras! I am loving it, Sombra!"

"Gumercindo had been talked into taking part in the ill-equipped revolution, Fierro."

"Montoneras were never well equipped, Sombra!"

"True, Fierro, but these men were armed mostly with home-made bamboo lances improvised from sheep-shearing scissors. These people were no match for government forces with firearms and cannons."

"Courage will overcome, Sombra! Believe me, it will!"

"Indeed, courage, and knowledge of the field, initially allowed these men to score a few fast victories, but they were encircled against the Uruguayan frontier."

"Encircled? That's bad, Sombra!"

"So bad, Fierro, that most abandoned the fight, the more professional army leaders first among them."

"Scoundrels! They are the worst, Sombra! I am telling you. Education emasculates!"

"It also gives one a better sense of opportunity, Fierro. In any case, Gumercindo's acquaintance with the field and his mounted men enabled him to inflict painful losses through montonera flash attacks, and he finally managed to lead his men to escape the encirclement."

"That's a gaucho, Sombra!"

"Indeed, Fierro! Gumercindo became a hero, and his standing in the revolution increased to the point of becoming an accepted military leader of an army of about three thousand Southern Brazilians who revolted against the still tender Brazilian Republic."[4]

> "When you are in a change management situation you cannot afford the slandering that will be slung at you. The more unified the voices are, the clearer the vision you want to convey. Republicans would never lose the opportunity to remind Brazilians that Gumercindo was no more than a Uruguayan-invading bandit."

[4] The rebellion lasted from 1893 to 1895 (Chasteen, 1995). The proclamation of the Brazilian republic took place in 1889.

"Now, that's a montonera! I never saw one as large as that, Sombra!"

"So large, Fierro, that it required organization, and a leader. Could Gumercindo deliver?"

"Of course, Sombra! If he amassed that following, he had it!"

"Yes, Fierro, no one can challenge that Gumercindo must have had charisma. What we need to ascertain is whether he had the organizational and communication skills that are required beyond the shouting stage."

"Of course he had that, too, Sombra! You know nothing of montoneras! Large montoneras are made of clusters of small montoneras, each one with a leader. The big montonera boss negotiates with the small montonera bosses who boss the rest around. The shouting stage is always with us. It's easy, Sombra!"

"Yes, and in a way it still is, but there is some evidence that Gumercindo could see further. Take for instance how he reassured his Brazilian followers of his intentions."

"They needed no reassurance, Sombra! They were already with him!"

"True, Fierro, many were, but what about those who had not yet joined? What about those on whose support he would have to rely in order to feed and shelter his followers? Gumercindo could not afford to alienate those, so he had to neutralize the badmouthing likely to come from the Republican quarters."

"Gumercindo's feat earned him the nickname of Pampa's Napoleon, which in many ways showed that Gumercindo was out of sync with his environment. Indeed, Gumercindo's significant advantage over military men had been his and his men's familiarity with the environment. But for many weeks he had been penetrating a world of mountains and boulders that was putting his horses and men to trial."

"The further away from his base, the faster he was losing his knowledge advantage. Under those circumstances one becomes insecure, susceptible. It's an uneasy feeling. Even though the knowledge advantage deficit was somewhat abated by the local knowledge brought in by those that joined in. That is how saladeros will expand in the future, bringing in competencies they lack, particularly when they expand abroad, which is what Gumercindo was doing."

"And how did he do that, Sombra?"

"When Gumercindo initially crossed borders into Brazil, with his three hundred mounted lancers, he issued a proclamation stating he was not an invader but a Brazilian patriot revolting against the unfairness of Republicans."[5]

"Why did he do that, Sombra?"

"Because, he was fighting for a Brazilian cause with a Uruguayan army."

"It was not a foreign army, Sombra! They were gauchos! Who can tell the difference between a gaucho here and a gaucho there!"

"Still, Fierro, when you are in a change management situation you cannot afford the slandering that will be slung at you. The more unified the voices are, the clearer the vision you want to convey. Republicans would never lose the opportunity to remind Brazilians that Gumercindo was no more than a Uruguayan-invading bandit."

"A courageous gaucho is never a bandit, Sombra!"

"I agree with you, Fierro, but Gumercindo eventually lost and was indeed depicted as a bandit, his memory vanished in Brazil. But, true, a bandit he was not. He was a significant landowner in eastern Uruguay and southern Brazil, where his ranching activities allowed him to offer a more than decent living to his wife and six children."

"There you are; he was a good man, Sombra!"

"Perhaps not altogether good, Fierro, but he must have been closer to a rural entrepreneur than a bandit. He was a doer, not an orator. He would leave the speechifying to others. He had little idea of what to do after victory if it came his way. He was out to wage war bound by the webs of loyalty. That was all."

"What's wrong with that, Sombra?"

"He lacked vision, Fierro. You can win battles without vision, but you cannot build anything without it!"

"Well, I am not so sure, Sombra. Did he need a vision? After all, he wanted to remove usurpers from government. Perhaps he

[5] As Saraiva was not prone to speaking in public, less so writing, the proclamation and perhaps even the idea for it may have originated in Saraiva's aide-de-camp, his medical doctor Angelo Dourado (Chasteen, 1995, 43).

only wanted to weed out the bad ones and leave the rest as they had found it. Do you need a vision for that?"

"Well, Fierro, Gumercindo was great, but his warring was holding history back. You had better have a vision if you want to do that. And he did not."

"I would leave the vision idea for those who want to create change, Sombra. Gumercindo wanted to support an Emperor. What is wrong with that?"

"Perhaps not so much with the Emperor as with the fact that it is hereditary, and that a cohort of sycophants tends to gravitate around the Emperor, which adds very little to the Emperor's effectiveness."

"Point well taken, Sombra. I am sure there also are a lot of fat asses hanging around the saladero bosses, adding little value to the jerked beef. Go ahead."

"The leader is fighting against insecurity all the time. After all, he is only human, Fierro. Though it could well be that they also have to be a bit mad. That is why in Curitiba people gathered at the train station to catch a glimpse of the Napoleon of the Pampas."

"In any case, Fierro, Gumercindo was not alone; Getúlio Vargas's father led troops, too. But it was Gumercindo who spearheaded his followers on horseback, about one thousand miles into Brazil, to the city of Curitiba."

"That was a long montonera, Sombra!"

"He must have been some leader, Fierro, but he fed on discontent."

"Every now and then the skeptic resurfaces in you, Sombra! Discontent? These people must have loved the excitement that joining Gumercindo's army offered! What kind of discontent is that?"

"Fierro, do you really believe men would leave their homes in droves to follow a man they did not know, offering them an elusive glory preceded by suffering and the likelihood of death?"

"Napoleon did just that, Sombra! And that is why we are here!"

"You are right, Fierro, and Gumercindo's feat earned him the nickname of Pampa's Napoleon, which in many ways showed that Gumercindo was out of sync with his environment. Indeed, Gumercindo's significant advantage over military men had been his and his men's familiarity with the environment. But for many weeks he had been penetrating a world of mountains and boulders that was putting his horses and men to trial."

"The further away from his base, the faster he was losing his knowledge advantage, Sombra, I know the feeling. One becomes insecure, susceptible. It's an uneasy feeling."

"True, Fierro, even though it was somewhat abated by the local knowledge brought in by those who joined in. That is how saladeros will expand in the future, bringing in competencies they lack, particularly when they expand abroad, which is what Gumercindo was doing."

"Sombra, why would a foreign organization want to attract locals to its ranks?"

"To reduce attrition, that is why Gumercindo initially issued that proclamation stating his was not a Uruguayan army taking over, remember? Many foreign corporations will operate in the same way."

"Wolves under a lamb's cloak?"

"Not really, Fierro, but it serves them better to appear as locals, who will feel more at ease in joining them, particularly if the alternatives are poor."

"Sombra, are you arguing that thousands joined Gumercindo's army because they were dissatisfied?"

"In short, yes."

"Dissatisfied with what, Sombra?"

"Brazil was undergoing important political changes since the liberation of slaves and the proclamation of the Republic—with the consequent shift of political power—and its currency was out of control. People were not happy and saw in Gumercindo's move a chance to bring things back to peace and stability."

> Gumercindo was a good leader to his men. He was so good he would recognize when he had reached his limit. He could no longer expect the support of a successful revolution in the capital city of Rio de Janeiro and could not hope to make it through the well-guarded Republican São Paulo that lied between his forces and Rio de janeiro. As Gumercindo initiated his withdrawal, he was ambushed and died from a cowardly gun-shot wound in southern Brazil. Heroes always die in ambushes. Cowards do not dare attack them face to face!

"So, dissatisfaction rather than love brought them in? Is that what you argue, Sombra?"

"Both played a role, Fierro, but with more of the first as a driver, I would say."

"If the need was already there, why would they join Gumercindo then and not anyone else, Sombra?"

"Ah, you've got a point there, Fierro! Gumercindo was a leader and he may have suppressed the sense of insecurity that was in the air. He certainly attracted a lot of attention; hordes gathered at the train station in Curitiba to see him upon arrival."

"He arrived by train?"

"Yes he did, Fierro. So many people had gathered at the station that Gumercindo had to have it cleared so he could have his wounded taken to hospital."

"Amazing, Sombra!"

"Indeed, Fierro. It was some feat. The man born and raised south of the frontier had become a hero to Brazilians."[6]

"Continue, Sombra, continue!"

"Unfortunately, there is not much more to tell."

"What do you mean; the man was greater than Facundo, for God's sake! Continue, Sombra."

"Fierro, Gumercindo would advance no more."

"Why not, Sombra?"

"Well, if he were to fight for Monarchism, he would have to topple the Republican government in São Paulo. Rio de Janeiro had been the seat of the Empire; there were plenty of Monarchists plotting there, but not enough to distract the Republican forces of São Paulo, which stood between Rio and Gumercindo's army."

"Why didn't they fight, Sombra?"

"Brazilians do not fight, Fierro."

"Cowards, are they?"

"No, Fierro, heirs of the Portuguese; they seek win-win solutions."

> "We all feel insecure at times; but leaders somehow overcome that basic insecurity, that is what makes them different. Followers can transfer their anxieties onto the chief, like to a totem."

[6] The people in the frontier region between Uruguay and Brazil had a common identity under separate jurisdictions (Chasteen, 1995, 106; Dobke, 2015, 90).

"As opposed to winner-take-all solutions, Sombra?"

"Precisely, Fierro. That is the most significant difference between the Brazilians and the rest of South Americans, who speak Spanish because they were colonized by Spain and were divided into feuding colonies, whereas Brazil remained united, in some ways like the United States."

"Why would the heirs of both Spain and Portugal, so close to each other in Europe, be so different in the New World?"

"Fierro, unlike the Spanish, the Portuguese found the way to the Indies and inserted themselves into a supply chain coming all the way from China. Consequently, the Portuguese became merchants, who tend to seek win-win solutions."

"What about the Spanish, Sombra?"

"They remained aristocratic and belligerent and transmitted their attitudes to the colonies in the New World."[7]

"So, Brazilians folded, Sombra. What else?"

"Fierro, Gumercindo was a good leader to his men. He was so good he could recognize when he had reached his limit. He could no longer expect the support of a successful revolution in the capital city of Rio de Janeiro and could not hope to make it through the well-guarded Republican São Paulo that lay between his forces and Rio.[8] As Gumercindo initiated his withdrawal, he was ambushed and died from a cowardly gunshot wound in Southern Brazil."

"Horrible, Sombra! Heroes always die in ambushes. Cowards do not dare attack them face to face! What next?"

"Gumercindo's death deflated the revolutionaries, Fierro. They buried him quickly and took the shortest route out of Brazil. His body was nonetheless exhumed and the government commander ordered his troops to march by the unearthed corpse so they would witness that the man was indeed dead. The government

[7] Behrens (2015, 214).

[8] Unlike Napoleon by 1814, Gumercindo Saraiva sensed his army would suffer defeat should he advance further, and so he withdrew at Curitiba. He saved his men, as would a humane leader of Canetti's crowd. Napoleon, instead, is remembered by Lewis Namier as "the man who in the past was able to gauge others, forestall them, lead them, or force them into his own ways, and who, above all men, knew the value of time, now began to lag behind events rather than meet and master them" (Namier, 1963, 4).

also ordered that he be left out of the grave to rot, and when he was buried eventually, the government had his corpse exhumed once more, beheaded, and his head taken to the Governor in Porto Alegre, for evidence as well as for research purposes."

"Beasts, Sombra! Gumercindo was fighting against beasts! Not only could they not face him with a facón, they would fail his memory, too!"

"Fierro, you know as well as I do that beheading was not an uncommon practice then. In an ammunition-short environment, knives were good enough to kill animals or men. Gauchos were used to slaughtering cattle and sheep by hanging them from their hind legs and bleeding them through cuts made into their necks."

"You may do that to cattle, Sombra! Not to heroes!"

"He was not a hero to those who defeated him, Sombra! Gumercindo's troops had beheaded many. Gumercindo's head would be the proof of his death."

"But if you do not censor that behavior, Sombra, it becomes legitimate!"

"You are right, Fierro! Elements of the Brazilian army fighting rural guerrillas in Araguaia are known to have beheaded adversaries as late as 1975. Chopping off the heads of their victims seems to have become part of the organizational memory."[9]

"It is akin to brutality, Sombra! It should not be condoned."

"Right you are, Fierro. Cruelty and brutality are to be stamped out under all circumstances. Upon Gumercindo's head arriving in Porto Alegre, the government's spokesperson is said to have stated:

> Wretched! May the earth that generously buries you weigh as much as the Andes ... and the memory of the bandit be damned forever.[10]

"Beasts, Sombra! Beasts! They had no sense of honor. That is all I can say! What did Gumercindo's followers do?"

"They fought for a few more weeks, Fierro, but they were on their way back; essentially they wound down the revolution. For a time."

[9] Dirceu (2005).

[10] Chasteen (1995, 2).

"Fair enough, but did they not vindicate Gumercindo's death?"

"It was a difficult time for them, Sombra. Republican efforts to testify to the death of Gumercindo were relentless, as well as a means to silence those who would question his death."

Brazilian Republicans suppressed Gumercindo, but not the latent dissatisfaction that had strengthened him. That dissatisfaction gave strength to a Messianic movement powered by opposition to the usurpation of land from poor peasants along a railway concession in Santa Catarina. That fueled what was called the War of the Contestado which lasted for four years, having started barely ten years after Gumercindo was beheaded. During that time the peasants fought with a rag-tag army of close to eight thousand peasants, more than half of which died.

"Gumercindo's followers could not believe it! That's right, Gumercindo did not die, and he lives in us!"

"In some ways you are right, Fierro. For many months the Monarchist combatants seemed to be wrapped up in Sebastianism, refusing to believe that Gumercindo was no longer with them; that he would not be able to lead them into another successful battle.[11] Rumors had it that he had only been wounded and was convalescing in Argentina from where he would soon return. Others claimed to have seen copies of war proclamations, or that Gumercindo's family had received a letter announcing his prompt return and that he had faked his death to confuse the enemy."[12]

"But he would not return; right, Sombra?"

"We are used to thinking that leaders are very assertive, even vociferous; but Gumercindo was not. He left the talking to his medical aid."

"That's right, Fierro, Gumercindo was dead. He had become a hero but his side had lost. To Monarchists, there was no one better than Gumercindo. His

[11] Sebastianism is rooted in the King in the mountain folk motif. The Portuguese reference, subsequently transported to Brazil, inspires people to wait for a hero to return to save them, as was expected of Portuguese King Sebastian, who had disappeared in the battle of Ksar El Kebir, 1578, Morocco (Suárez, 1991).

[12] Chasteen (1995,111).

medic aide-de-camp, Angelo Dourado, reported that Gumercindo was gentle with his men when needing support but relentless in punishing indiscipline, like when he ordered the execution of one of his men upon molesting a female civilian in Curitiba. He ordered his whole regiment to march at the side of the corpse of the offending soldier to rub in Gumercindo's distaste for abuse."[13]

"He was a good man, Sombra! And he was beheaded in death; it is outrageous!"

"True, Fierro, but for all his merits, Gumercindo would be forgotten in Brazil. In a new Republic, where a national image was being painfully put together, there was no room for a defeated Federalist who had fought with Monarchist supporters. Even among the latter, there cannot have been much interest in insisting on cherishing a leader who would prevent the healing. Gradually, Gumercindo's image withered. There are no equestrian statues of him, no plaques, no poetry, nothing. His image completely vanished, where, barely more than a century prior, he led about three thousand men almost two thousand miles into the heartland of Brazil! Gumercindo vanished to the extent that in the largest Brazilian city, São Paulo, there is just a small street with his name, only a hundred meters long."

"Sad, Sombra! Very sad! His feats should be chanted by all. Did it all end like that, so sadly?"

"Not really, the Republicans suppressed Gumercindo, but not the latent dissatisfaction that had strengthened him. That gave strength to a Messianic movement powered by opposition to the usurpation of land from poor peasants along a railway concession in Santa Catarina (still in Southern Brazil though not as far south). That gave place to what was called the War of the Contestado, which started barely ten years after Gumercindo was beheaded and lasted for four years. During that time the peasants fought with a rag-tag army of close to eight thousand peasants, more than half of whom died."[14]

[13] Chasteen (1995, 114).

[14] Machado (2007).

"I see your point, Sombra; there was an undercurrent that fed Gumercindo's advance."

"And it was all across the country, Fierro. Gumercindo's campaign followed the suppression of Canudos that sprang up in the Northeast."

"What was that, Sombra?"

"Another Messianic movement, this one led by Antonio Conselheiro, defeated on the fourth attempt after an artillery bombardment. More than five thousand houses were blown up by the Republican army."

"Cowards, Sombra! Cowards once and again! I am incensed, Sombra! Incensed!"

The Suppression of the Canudos movement, of the Federalist revolution and the War of Contestado demonstrates Brazilian intolerance. There is little advantage to Brazilian size, if managing that size requires total acquiescence and the intolerant suppression of diversity. This is something for managers to think about at large companies, because intolerance is anathema to creativity.

"Fierro! Conselheiro and the self-appointed monks at Contestado were leaders in that they had followers. But what else did they have?"

"What did the jerks that killed them have going for them? Tell me, Sombra! Were they superior, or did they have superior arms and no judgment in how to use them?"

"You may be right again, Fierro. A reporter who could not be accused of being pro-Conselheiro was also scathing toward the army commander of the third expedition, Colonel Moreira César.[15]

"So there, Sombra! The leaders at Canudos and Contestado had courage and followers! Is that not enough? Why could they not have been left alone? Is this country not large enough for all?"

[15] Referred to as "his diminutive appearance exhausted itself in thin legs reminding reminiscent of parentheses, altogether giving the impression he was unfit for the career he had chosen for himself" (Cunha, 1968, 222).

Aparício was known to be loved by his soldiers. He was also admired for his skills with horses and the facón and for taking part on cavalry attacks, actually leading the attacks himself. He would also share his food with his soldiers and visit them at night at their campfires. A bit like Shakespeare tells us of Henry V, who secretly listened to the anxieties of his men before the battle of Agincourt and later echoed their feelings in his St. Crispin's Day Speech.

"You are right in that, Fierro. But communications were poor and the Republican bosses were not in the mood to tolerate deviant movements. Perhaps they were afraid, too, and did not want the example to spread, which could have fragmented the country, as happened to the Spanish colonies."

"Death must be the price to pay for dignity, Sombra."

"Death might be too high a price to pay for it, even when the dying is suffered by the other, Fierro."

"What do you mean by that?"

"Fierro, the time will come when Argentines will have killed seventy times more of their lot than Brazilians did for similar reasons.[16] Despite the bloodshed, they will not be better off, in terms of dignity or otherwise."

"How so?"

"Fierro, Argentine grandparents will spend the rest of their lives looking for the kidnapped babies borne of their children who were killed while captive."

Fierro crossed himself in silence. "What is the advantage of size, Sombra, if Brazil will not tolerate diversity?"

"You are right again, Fierro."

"Well, you had better do some hard thinking, Sombra! Because if death is to become the price of attempts at innovation, it will take this place a hell of a long time before they invent anything!"

Fierro was irate, brandishing his facón in his right hand and pointing it to the heavens while he rode in eights on Spinoza, who would occasionally stand on his hind legs and neigh: "*At politici*

[16] The Argentine national anthem is considerably more aggressive than the Brazilian anthem; as a share of their populations during their dirty wars, death was much higher among Argentines than Brazilians (Behrens, 2015).

*contra hominibus magis insidiari, quam consulere creduntur, et potius callidi, quam sapientes aestimantur.*"[17]

## Lesson: The Rehashing of Leadership When the Situation Changes

After he had calmed down a bit, Fierro continued, "But, Sombra, let us go back to the story of my personal hero, Gumercindo. What happened to his brother, Aparício, after he was beheaded?"

"There is a twist, Fierro. Aparício's story is different. He was younger and known to be more humorous than Gumercindo. Aparício followed his older brother into war, earned considerable respect with his cavalry and spear charges, and was renowned for having impaled two Republican soldiers in one lancer's blow. He continued fighting for as long as he could to avenge his slain brother and managed to escape and made it back to Uruguay."

"Well, that is the least he could have done. What next, Sombra?"

"Aparício was known to be loved by his soldiers. He was also admired for his skills with horses and the knife and for taking part in cavalry attacks, actually leading the attacks himself. He would also share his food with his soldiers and visit them at night at their campfires.[18] A bit like Shakespeare tells us of Henry V, who secretly listened to the anxieties of his men before the Battle of Agincourt and later echoed their feelings in his St. Crispin's Day speech."[19]

"Clever of him, Sombra! That kid knew how to keep in touch with his men and relieve them of their fears, by making them his own![20] He turned himself into a totem! Very clever!"

[17] "But statesmen, on the other hand, are suspected of plotting against mankind, instead of consulting their interests, and are believed to be more crafty than learned." Spinoza (1667, Intro para 2). See https://ebooks.adelaide.edu.au/s/spinoza/benedict/political/. Accessed January 2, 2017.

[18] Chasteen (1995, 157).

[19] "We few, we happy few, we band of brothers; / For he to-day that sheds his blood with me / Shall be my brother; be he ne'er so vile.' (Shakespeare, Henry V, c1599, Act 4, Scene 3).

[20] "Before the battle, even the general seeks intimacy with his lowest subordinates… It conveys a feeling of equality … despite the extreme hierarchy of the military" (Roy, 2001,195).

"Yes, Fierro. Whatever his Colorado detractors may say, Aparício was a leader. Most men can give orders. Many fewer can give orders that will be followed. Aparício was a bit like you, too."

"In what sense, Sombra?"

"He enjoyed a fight. In October 1895, a Uruguayan reporter was interviewing him at his estancia, sipping mate from Saravia's own gourd, and asked him whether there was any grounding in the comments that he was considering taking on Montevideo, whose rulers were ideologically closer to the Brazilians he had fought against across the frontier. Aparício was very dismissive, arguing that a Uruguayan who loved his country should forget about revolutions. Yet, shortly after, as he resumed riding on horseback, he pulled the reins of his horse to make a stop and, looking at the countryside, sighed to the same reporter: "What a beautiful place for a battle! After one takes a liking for it, it is quite fun!"[21]

"Aha! Sombra! You see! That is a man! He knows he can die, but he does not care! Too much attachment to life turns a man into a coward."

"Indeed, Fierro! Aparício may have offered his men some thrills, at least in the ways that bond men together for attack."

"Nothing is wrong with that, believe me! To hell with civilization, Sombra!"

"Watch it, Fierro, you may soon begin to sound like the Taliban, Khmer Rouge, the Islamic State, the Shining Path, Brexit or America First."

"What are those?"

"Periodic resurgences of xenophobic nativism, Fierro, not more than that."

> Gumercindo was very careful when entering Brazil, issuing that cautionary proclaim. He spelled out the purpose, and excused himself for intruding with a foreign contingent. They might have looked familiar, but essentially, they were foreigners. Gumercindo had to be careful not to stir-up the xenophobic response. Gumercindo was almost asking for permission, offering help; even though it was a takeover. Gumercindo was making an entry into a territory controlled by the competition and he could not afford to stir up too much opposition at a time he was weak.

[21] Chasteen (1995, 179).

"Sombra! Don't you get it?"

"Of course I do, Fierro. I can even understand that some leaders may be invested with supernatural powers by their followers, even have unusual anatomy: Aparício was said to have three testicles instead of only two like most of us."[22]

"There you are, Sombra! Perhaps he did, too!"

"Fierro, Aparício would be less of a commander than Gumercindo, but probably more beloved. He appears to have been a more attractive symbol than Gumercindo. This may have led to the turnaround in Aparício's career in Uruguay, an extension of his fate in Southern Brazil."

"So, Aparício went back to Uruguay? Just as well if he was keen on holding onto his head!"

"Indeed, Fierro, when Uruguay's Blanco Party, the Oribe one, was seeking a figure around whom to coalesce their strength, Aparício was brought onto the scene and he became the best-known Blanco leader across the country."

"It doesn't surprise me, Sombra! Good for him, as long as he did not sell out to the educated elite who would only want to use him as a logo."

"He was useful to the Blancos, Fierro. He had the fighting credentials and he stood for the strength of the nativist proclivities of the Blanco Party at a time when the urbanite Colorado Party was showing greater response to the waves of immigrants' ideas."

> There are styles that may appeal more readily to some individuals than to others. There may have to be an alignment with a cause and a style of leadership. Christians may not have followed Christ had he been a vociferous leader.

"So, the Blancos were not as interested in his fighting skills as in his fighting profile? It is like buying an all-terrain vehicle just to use in the streets!"

"Sombra, the nativist ideal, the 'return to the roots' attitude of the Blanco Party, was a script in search of a character; this is how

[22] Heard by the author from an old combatant of Aparicio Saravia. Author's diaries, Mercedes, Uruguay, January 6, 1967.

Aparício became the embodiment of the myth and was rapidly accepted as such, despite having been little known to Blanco Party members prior to 1896, and despite his cultural differences, for Aparício could have easily been taken for a Brazilian.[23]

"OK. But did Aparício fight again?"

"Oh, yes he did, Fierro! And he was scary, too!"

"Good for him, Sombra!"

"The myth the Blancos alluded to was advanced largely by the prolific pen of the Uruguayan Eduardo de Acevedo Diaz. He appealed to virile self-sacrifice and shared images like those Aparício had offered in his Brazilian campaign."

The alignment of the leader's vision and style must be echoed in the recruitment.

"Nonsense! Sombra, the only true orgy takes place during a montonera attack!"

## Lessons: Authentic Leadership, Communication, Recruitment, Sense of Timing

"Sombra, this has been a long montonera. What do we have at hand here?"

"This has been a great lesson, Fierro. Gumercindo was undoubtedly a leader in that people followed him."

"There is no better indication of leadership, Sombra!" He started off with three hundred and reached a peak of three thousand fighters while two thousand miles away from home!"

"Indeed, Fierro. Quite a feat!"

"There is also the issue of his style, Sombra."

"In what sense, Fierro?"

"He left the talking to his doctor."

"True, I found that strange, perhaps because he was not the type you would immediately follow. You like the shouting leaders, Fierro."

"Nothing is wrong with that, Sombra."

[23] Chasteen (1995,133).

"True, but Fierro, it would have been hard to fit the message of love in a shout! Gumercindo's message was conservative; he was fighting for the restoration of imperial order, which goes with subdued manners, does it not, Fierro?"

"Yes, not my style, but a leader nonetheless, Sombra."

"Precisely, Fierro. And the alignment of vision and style must be echoed in the recruitment."

"How, Sombra?"

"Well, think of it, Fierro. Where did Gumercindo do his recruiting?"

"In the countryside, Sombra. Why was that?"

"Because it would cost him less to persuade potential followers there, Fierro."

"Why?"

"City people are more modern, they attach more swiftly to new ideas, like Republicanism."

"Yes, it's Neapolitan."

"Not only is it Neapolitan, but city people would hold values different from his own. Some of Gumercindo's efforts would have been wasted in the cities, so he recruited in the countryside."

In hiring from the market, unlike Gumercindo who recruited teams from the countryside, the saladeros will expect top team performance from groups of people that are not teams because they were hired individually.

"Well, it is rather obvious, is it not?"

"It will be forgotten, Fierro."

"How?"

"Saladero managers will attempt to seek like-minded individuals at top universities without bearing in mind that there is not enough challenge in jerking beef to hold a top-university graduate in the business for long."

"Why would the saladero managers do that, Sombra?"

"Saladero managers will be risk avoiders, Fierro."

"Cowards, you mean?"

"Perhaps not that bad, but in recruiting graduates from top universities they think they will avoid criticism."

"A bit foolish, is it not, to hire Neapolitan-speaking candidates when they could do just as well if not even better with an honest illiterate gaucho?"

At Latinbeef, the managers asked their best workers if they had people to recommend. Latinbeef then issued each good worker with a numbered token and had a draw, selecting the amount of tokens roughly equal to the number of new people they wanted to hire. In addition, Latinbeef told the good workers that they would be responsible for the quality of the people they recommended. Latinbeef rewarded their most engaged workers and extended their attitude by allowing them to select and sponsor the new hires, which also results in faster teambuilding.

"Saladero managers will think they will look bad hiring gauchos to jerk beef. They will want top university graduates, to look good. They will put advertisements in the papers requiring competencies that might not even be needed for the job, but will look good on paper."

"Isn't that like lying, Sombra?"

"Only a bit, Fierro. But the result will be that young and competent graduates will not stay with them for long."

"Thank goodness they won't, Sombra!"

"Worse than that, Fierro."

"How can it get worse?"

"In hiring from the market, unlike Gumercindo, who recruited teams from the countryside, the saladeros will expect top team performance from groups of people who do not easily form teams because they were hired individually."

"How silly of saladero managers, Sombra. We learned that when we observed the formation of legions according to nationality during the Siege of Montevideo. Where will the saladero managers get those fancy ideas from?"

"From foreign textbooks, Fierro."

"I knew it would be Neapolitan!"

"Whether Neapolitan or not, it will be a waste, Fierro, and will lead to a lot of frustration."

"Is there no better way to run saladeros, Sombra?"

"Of course, every now and then a streak of wisdom ignites, like in Latinbeef, not far away from here, in Taubaté, São Paulo."

"Tell me more, Sombra."

"Latinbeef was a phenomenal saladero that spread from Argentina to Brazil and Portugal, owned by foreigners who were big at saladeros in Detroit."[24]

The leader must have good sensing and positioning skills to tell when the game is over; when it was time to withdraw to save the lives of his men.

"Bad ones, Sombra?"

"People who wanted Latinbeef to succeed, which is what counts."

"Go ahead, Sombra."

"For years Latinbeef had been scaling down operations, but circumstances changed and they found themselves needing to hire again."

"Good or bad, Sombra?"

"Good, is it not?"

"I mean, did they go the usual way, putting ads in the papers and selecting people from the best schools?"

"No, Fierro, this time they did the right thing; they distributed tokens among their best workers entitling them to recommend an entry-level worker whose performance they would remain responsible for."

"Not a bad idea, Sombra! I've always contended that a facón clears people's minds, even mindless workers at saladeros!"

"Indeed, Fierro! The workers would then choose to sponsor the relatives or friends who would make them look best."[25]

"What else did we learn from Gumercindo, Sombra?"

"We had a change management situation here, didn't we, Fierro?"

[24] The northern reader may be bewildered by the use of the eighteenth-century Latin American term saladeros to refer to modern corporations. However, while Fierro and Sombra were roaming across Latin America, Upton Sinclair (1906) was denouncing the American meatpacking industry in *The Jungle.* As late as 2017, Justin Fox was musing over similar issues at Bloomberg View: "Low-Pay Jobs Boom in the Slaughterhouse."

[25] I am indebted to Fernando Perez for this piece of practical experience in a car-manufacturing plant with more than 40,000 workers.

"Ambushes are the only way you can get rid of heroes, Fierro. Because heroes don't give up and cowards to not dare face them!"

"At least one in the making, Sombra."

"True, it did not become a full change management situation because it was thwarted at Curitiba. But all along it was one, with an invasion included."

"Invasion my foot, Sombra! Gumercindo's men were not foreigners, they were gauchos, too! The same thing on both sides of the frontier!"

"But they would have looked like foreigners to the Republicans in São Paulo, Fierro."

"But those were too far North to worry about at the time Gumercindo came in from the South, Sombra."

"Fierro, Republicans had put down the empire and they had allies in the South who looked very much like the ones in São Paulo. Gumercindo was making an entry into a territory controlled by the enemy, and he could not afford to stir up too much opposition at a time when he was weak."

"Yes, you are right, Sombra, it was clever of him to enter with a humble attitude. Was it a fake?"

"It is unlikely, from such a reserved man. It was quite likely straight talk from an authentic leader. Otherwise he would not have been so effective at recruiting."

"What else did we learn, Sombra?"

"That the leader must have good sensing and positioning skills to tell when the game is over, Fierro. When it was time to withdraw to save the lives of his men."

"I did not like that part so much."

"But he spared the lives of his men, Fierro."

"True, but he got himself killed, nonetheless; he could have died fighting, Sombra."

"Gumercindo had not surrendered, Fierro, he was only retreating."

"It amounts to the same thing, Sombra!"

It is only up to God to tell who is worth more: The heroes, or the cowards that order their deaths in ambushes. But surely I would prefer to work with authentic leaders than with the scarecrows of them.

"It surely does not, Fierro! He had hopes while he was alive. He could have made a comeback at a more auspicious time. That is why they killed him, to put an end to the threat."

"At an ambush, too, Sombra. How cowardly of them!"

"It is the only way you can get rid of heroes, Fierro. Because they don't give up!"

"But are they not worth more than the cowards who order their deaths in ambushes?"

"Fierro, it is only up to God to tell who is worth more; but for sure, I would prefer to work with authentic leaders than those pretending to be authentic."

"But you see, Fierro, in sparing his men, Gumercindo gave life to a new war, or the same one with different scenery—the war of his younger brother, Aparício, in Uruguay."

"True, Sombra. It was wise of him to retreat at Curitiba. And what about the beheading of Gumercindo's corpse? Let us not forget about that!"

"Well, it is the expression of brutes, is it not, Fierro? Contrast that with the proclamation Gumercindo issued when entering Brazil. Brutes talk death, dishonorable death, too, and it will resurface when combating guerrillas in the Araguaia eight decades later. Organizations have long memories, Sombra; bad memories especially linger. This is why it pays to force authenticity into them, so that it prevails, and workers know for sure what they are fighting for and what is expected from them. Doubletalk kills an organization."

# 7

# The Unquenchable Thirst for Honor: The Bullfight

> Bullfighting is the only art in which the artist is in danger of death and in which the degree of brilliance in the performance is left to the fighter's honor.
>
> – Ernest Hemingway, *Death in the Afternoon,* 1932

Fierro and Sombra arrived in Caracas, which they look upon from El Ávila Mountain. They watched the Nuevo Circo—the bullfighting plaza, so large that when inaugurated, in 1919 by President Gómez, it could house a considerable share of Caracas' inhabitants.[1]

"Fierro, is there anything heavenly in bullfighting or is it plain butchery?" asked Sombra, with a half grin on his face as he idly looked into the Valley of Caracas's bullfighting arena.

"Now there, Sombra, who's the provocateur now?"[2]

"Well, Fierro, what is bullfighting? A leftover of a savage pagan belief, or is there a contemporary meaning to it?"

"Sombra, bullfighting may not be Catholic, in that it is not part of the ritual any more than Rio de Janeiro's Carnival is, but like Carnival, bullfighting is defined by the Catholic calendar. It is the most Spanish of all fiestas."

"So, it's a party, Fierro. A hell of a party for the bull!"

[1] More on Juan Vicente Gómez in Chapter 8.

[2] So far in this narrative, the more rational, calculating Sombra has taken the role of the instructor. In this chapter, the passionate Fierro becomes the protagonist and the role of emotions in social transformation is highlighted.

"Sombra, a fiesta it is. In Spain, bullfights can be staged after marriages—for it is a fertility rite—and always after Mass, never before, and always between Easter and the end of summer."

"So, it is not religious, Fierro, but would it exist without religion?"

"Call it the *fiesta brava*, Sombra, in opposition to Mass, the *fiesta mansa*. The fiesta brava can be seen as a toning down of an excess of beatitude after the cleansing spirit of the sacrifice of the lamb.[3] Too much meekness, as expressed by 'turning the other cheek' would lead to the wicked taking over."

"For a fiesta it looks pretty wicked to me already, Fierro."

"Sombra, bullfighting transforms the Catholic ritual diet into a festival of manliness."

"I cannot see much manliness in an effeminate man slaughtering a tired and weakened bull, Fierro!"

"Sombra, you know many things but it shows that, in taking an aesthetically pleasing performance for effeminacy, you do not know much about manliness or bullfighting!"

"I am willing to learn, Fierro."

"Bullfighting, like so many rituals, can serve many meanings, Sombra, yet over time one has been predominant: the celebration of virility."

"Repetition does not make it more credible, Fierro!"

"Sombra, this is deep, listen! The bull represents the courage, aggressiveness, straightforwardness, nobility and—last though not least—the potency necessary for reproduction inherent in man. This is why those, like priests, who claim to be closer to God—implicitly further from the beast—display celibacy vows."

"*Sacre bleu*, Fierro! You've gone too far now. Come back to full-blown men, will you?"

"What does the bullfight consist of, Sombra? It is a ritual in three stages called *tercios*. During the first tercio, the virgin bull—because he never has been fought before—enters the arena in all his power, head up."

[3] In the times of Abraham, the lamb was a valued possession, its sacrifice entailed a loss intended for the common good. On the other hand, "the sacrifice of the bull restores to grace the mores of everyday life" (Pitt-Rivers, 1993, 12).

"Yes, Fierro. The bull leaves his kennel alive, powerful; he may disgorge a couple of horses—or they used to, until the horses were protected! That's what bulls do. Those are the bulls the matador should fight. Like you did against the *moreno*, remember?" Sombra continued, quoting a stanza of the Martín Fierro poem "*Caballeros, dejen venir ese toro. Solo nací—solo muero* ('Gentlemen, let that bull charge. Alone I was born, alone I might die.')."[4]

"Of course I remember my story, Sombra, but this is another one; there is a script to be enacted: The bull must be killed, honorably, with one blow; a sword through his heart."

"So, Fierro, no Colt? No Smith & Wesson? No Winchester?"

"No, Sombra. I said honorably, facing the bull, close enough for the bull to have a chance to kill the matador."

"Why?"

"Because the matador must prove he is manly enough to risk them."

"Risk what?"

"His genitals, Sombra, no less!"

"What do you mean, Fierro?"

"It works like this, Sombra, the bull's head must be lowered if the fighter is to have any chance at all of putting the bull out with one blow of a short spade—in the third tercio, the death tercio (*el tercio de la muerte*)."

"So?"

"So, during the first tercio the *picador*, mounted on a horse and armed with a spear, will aim his weapon to the bull's muscles that prop the head up. If he is perceived to overdo his job, the picador is booed by the crowd which anticipates an uneven fight."

> "The effrontery of the suit of lights, its tight-hugging breeches, the flaunting of the male sex organ, the importance given to the buttocks, the obviously seductive and self-appraising stride, the lust for blood and sensation—the bullfight authorizes this incredible arrogance and sexual exhibitionism." The Buried Mirror (Fuentes, 1993, 2)

[4] In stanza 205, Fierro narrates his duel against a dark-skinned man whose wife he had insulted. Fierro alludes to the man's strength, similar to that of a charging bull, while Fierro defies death by comparing to another passage, like birth (Hernández, 1936).

"They always overdo it, Fierro."

"Nonsense, if they did, the aficionados would stop attending. It is fair play."

"I don't agree, but continue, Fierro."

"The second tercio is another stage of the tiring of the bull. The *banderillas*—beribboned barbed spears—are placed in the bull's neck by the matador himself."

"What for?"

"That is the reckoning stage. Each bull is unique and all have different ways of attacking, which the matador must figure out early enough to avoid being gored by the bull and before he attempts to kill the bull in one blow."

"But why the banderillas, Fierro?"

"Sombra, the whole purpose is to get close enough to the bull, to risk your life at it; and the banderillas hanging from the bull's rump are the proof of that risky proximity!"

"Some proof!"

"Sombra, placing one's flag has been man's way of signaling his presence for ages! I would not doubt that the day man lands on the moon they will leave a flag there to signal their presence!"

"Forget the moon; focus on the bull, Fierro!"

"The last tercio is the one of death, Sombra. The ritual has reached its climax. Bull and matador are in the arena to penetrate each other."

"Getting interesting!"

"It is very erotic, Sombra! Carlos Fuentes will recognize that bullfighting in the New World entices erotic feelings very similar to those alluded to in Spain and Portugal."[5]

"OK, OK. Fierro, it's only poetry, continue."

"Sombra! Each time the bull's horn passes a thumbspace away

> "What the script requires is that the matador put his masculinity at stake. If all works well for the matador, the bull will have been defiled. The bull will bleed to an immediate death and the blood so drawn will have transferred the bull's masculinity to the matador, whose honor will thus have been preserved. The bull will be dead, and in being dead it will have lost its own masculinity. So goes the saying: *Toro muerto, vaca es* ('The dead bull becomes a cow')."

[5] "Bullfighting is, lest we forget, also an erotic event" (Fuentes, 1999, 22).

from the body of the matador, men and women's lower bowel muscles tense in expectation of the goring. Georges Bataille will one day claim that women have orgasms at the repeated passes of the bull's horns a thumbspace away from the matador!"[6]

"Don't believe anything Bataille will say!"

"Yet risky as the passes are, each pass builds the matador's understanding of the details of the bull's response. If the matador is to kill the bull with only one blow, it will have to be with a downward stroke in the middle of his back."

"Some feat!"

"Precisely, Sombra! The matador needs to reckon the bull's attack style in order to learn how to lead the bull to align its forefeet while the head is low."

"Why, Fierro?"

"Because only then will the bull's shoulder blades open passage for the matador's spade into his heart, leading to the bull's immediate, ennobling, death."

"But the matador's arm is too short for that, Fierro!"

"Precisely, Sombra! The matador will have to jump over the bull's head and use his body weight to thrust the sword down to the bull's heart!"

"My goodness, Fierro! If in that moment the bull raises its head, his horns will gore the matador in his genitalia!"

"You've got it, Sombra! That is why that moment when the matador leans over the bull's head is called the 'moment of truth'! It is the most dangerous move of the entire fiesta!"

"So the script requires that the matador be gored precisely where his masculinity is at stake, Fierro?"

"Not really, Sombra; what the script requires is that the matador put his masculinity at stake. If all works well for the matador, the bull will have been defiled. The bull will bleed to an immediate death and the blood so drawn will have transferred the bull's masculinity to the matador, whose honor will thus have been preserved. The bull will be dead, and in being dead it will have lost its own masculinity. So goes the saying: *Toro muerto, vaca es* ('The dead bull becomes a cow')."

[6] Bataille sees sexual orgasm as coming slowly for the female but often for the male with fulminating force, two beings projected onto each other beyond their limits (Bataille, 1962, 103; 1979, 70).

"A hell of a way to prove your masculinity, Sombra!"

"Sombra, it is not really the matador's masculinity that is at stake, it is the matador's honor, through his masculinity. That is the essence of the ritual, because without honor life is not worth living!"

"Nonsense, Sombra! That is very *ancien régime*!"

"Yet it prevails, Fierro! Philippe d'Iribarne will pick it up in management![7] If it were all about masculinity, why would the man dress up so effeminately?"

"Sombra!" Fierro reproached him. "Like Aeschylus's fox, you may know a little about a lot of things, but about manhood I can teach you a lesson or two. A matador is one hell of a man, whatever he chooses to wear!"

"OK, OK, Fierro! Don't get so worked up!"

"Sombra!" Fierro was speaking straight into Sombra's face. "The matador's dress is a second skin, and it is designed to emphasize his body line, his firm buttocks and his ballet-like movements. All—the heat, the sweat, the abundance in the bull's potency, the bright sunlight that enlivens the colors, the transparency in the authenticity of the matador, the intensity in the crowd's unison *olés!* with their joint sense of belonging—all add to the pleasure in the tension of the passes that lead to the moment of truth!"[8]

"Yes, yes, I see it!"

"You say you see it, Sombra, but do you? Can you also, intimately, ardently see it? Can you see why the lack of that delicate balance was what that led to the prohibition of bullfighting in the higher-latitude countries, like Argentina and Uruguay, though they once did have their bullfighting arenas?"

"What are you talking about now, Fierro?"

"You see, you still do not get it, Sombra! It also takes the sun—its heat and its light—to produce a proper bullfight! It is a ritual to be carried out between the forty-plus degrees of latitude, between North and South. Beyond that, it is not the same thing! Caracas has the sunlight one needs!"

7 Philippe D'Iribarne (1989) portrays honor as a driving force in management among the French, suggesting that the French aristocratic tradition still today permeates the relationship between managers and workers.

8 Fuentes (1999, 22).

Fierro raises his voice as if speaking to the Gods, "Because you need the heat and the yellow-red hues that go with it. You need the people's extraversion, the sense of communion, like in a Canetti crowd, to cry *olé* together while you tighten your crotch in fear of losing it! Because you need the blinding light that will cut off the black bull's silhouette when he first enters the arena: all fury, power, potency and aggressiveness. All resides with the unflappable bull, while the fragile and effeminately dressed matador attracts and defies the bull, just as woman challenges man. I am still not sure you get it, Sombra! You are too rational for it! But I am having one hell of a time!"

"OK, Fierro!"

"Don't you OK me, Sombra! I am not done yet!"

"Then comes the progressive subjugation of the beast, through the spearing, the passes, the *olés!* Until the final moment!"

"The moment of truth, Fierro, I got it!"

"Yes, Sombra," Fierro spoke softly, "When the matador in his arched glittering body removes the sword form the bright red cape and raises it to the sky before penetrating the bull!" Fierro, relaxed. "The ritual ends with the new man and the audience satiated once more, reassured of the reinstating of social order and the subjugation of the women, taken to be capable of depriving the man of his honor."

"Game over, Fierro!"

## Leadership Lessons from Bullfighting

I now explain why bullfighting, inasmuch as it is a cultural expression, also expresses the symbolic association of courage and leadership.

Bullfighting is a ritual whose reenactment over the centuries has allowed it to be analyzed. This analysis can be both completed and contested. For instance, a deeper understanding of the inner drive behind the behavior of

> Perhaps the most important lesson to be drawn is that bullfighting expresses the lack of pragmatism in the societies where it is practiced. There is an almost anti-utilitarian purpose in bullfighting. That repudiation of pragmatism confers strength to the seeking of transcendence valued by the leader's followers. The matador is admired for taking the risk he does. That admiration is the one the workers are likely to be ready to bestow on the business leader, if he proves worthy of it.

the matador would help. But that work, as with most men exposed to public scrutiny, is not inclined to introspective pursuits. At least that is the regret of Cecílio Paniagua, a medical doctor who found only one psychoanalytic rendition of the therapeutic treatment of a matador, who—incidentally—was a failed matador.[9]

First of all, bullfighting is an important cultural expression on account of its longevity. Spain, as well as much of Portugal, Southern France and many New World countries, espouse, in the ritual of the bullfight, much of the honor code demonstrated in the sport. These societies are riddled with the notion of honor and even weakened by the stress of its loss, if even for fickle behavior. Yet the observance of the honor code is both a painful and a restless source of agreed-upon and cohesive social behavior.

In the Spanish New World one can repeatedly find similar seemingly nonsensical displays of courage for little or no gain. Such is the case of the Acapulco plungers, for instance, or of Che Guevara's life in revolution, Fidel's 1962 suicidal gamble, or of President Allende's fatal resistance to General Pinochet's onslaught on Allende's Presidential mandate.

> At the time of the Russian missile crisis of 1962, Fidel Castro offered the Russian Premier, if needs be, to fire the nuclear missiles on the United States first, even if this meant the annihilation of Cuba in an expected American retaliation. Castro was running the bullfighter's cape on the United States at a time that restraint may have worked to America's disadvantage. Castro's defiance of several American governments expressed the Latin leader's rejection of pragmatism.

The Acapulco plungers climb a cliff to dive into a shallow cove during the time it takes for the surf to make it somewhat deeper. The climbing of the cliff itself is dangerous enough, not to mention the diving into the cove. Yet the divers have been reenacting this ritual for decades, and for a pittance—if one were to ignore the value of the recognition of the divers in their own community, where their performance can be seen as a ritual of self-transcendence.

Similarly, the Cuban defiance of several American governments

[9] "Sadistic gratification is seen as bullfighting's main attraction, with perceived danger to the bullfighter an essential source." Thus the drama of a failed matador (Paniagua, 1994).

is an expression of lack of pragmatism, to the point of almost provoking a nuclear holocaust in 1962. Che Guevara's behavior is no less daring. Having left Argentina on a soul-searching adventure, he joined the Cuban revolution and collaborated with the tough initial decisions there. But Guevara was not made to endure routine. He would join Congo rebels, and subsequently in Bolivia met the death with which he had long been fighting. But he had told a Russian KGB emissary that if there were a conflict that they would lose, not to look for him among the exiles in a foreign embassy. To look for him among the dead.[10]

Similarly, for Chilean President Allende when his Presidential palace was being bombed by Pinochet's forces on September 11, 1975. President Allende must have known he would not survive. But perhaps he intuitively knew his life would not be spared at any rate, so he decided to put on a show: he would die defending his legitimate mandate.

A pursuit of glory may also be an individual quest. Take, for instance, the renowned Uruguayan soccer player Abdón Porte, some ten years after Aparício Saravia's glorious reentry into Uruguayan politics. In 1918, Abdón was still a good player, but—at twenty-five—he could already see that soon he would become a has-been.

One evening, after celebrating a well-deserved soccer victory with his team, Abdón returned to his team's football field near midnight, and standing in the middle of the field he put a bullet into his heart. His corpse was discovered by his team's goalkeeper the next morning. By his corpse lay Abdón's straw hat, a revolver, and two letters: a farewell to his family and another farewell to his loving team, Nacional.[11] In the latter, like Costa Rica's Juan

> Abdón Porte, the famed Uruguayan football player, chose to depart in the apex of his career, committing suicide at age 25 in his team's field. There was little purpose for Abdón in lingering if his team was his *raison d'être*. Spilling his blood for his team expressed trustworthy evidence of his detachment from material gain and of his loyalty to his followers.

[10] Gielow (2008).

[11] This episode inspired stories by at least two famed Uruguayan writers, Galeano "El fútbol a sol y sombra" and Quiroga "Juan Polti, half back" (Clarin, 2015).

Santamaria, Abdón Porte asked his team leaders to see to his mother.

Almost a century has passed, and when Nacional plays one may still see banners carried by Nacional supporters with sayings such as "for Abdón's blood."

Such is the price of honor in Latin societies; it boils down to matters of life and death. Facing such odds ensures that self-transcendence is pursued; for that seems to be the motive, at least since Roman times, as we have seen among the gladiators. But let us return to bullfighting, because the bullfighter is not a gladiator; perhaps he is a duelist? After all, when Polish-born Joseph Conrad wrote *The Duel*, where did he choose to stage the obsessive saga that opposed the lieutenants of a regiment of hussars, Féraud against D'Hubert?[12] It was in France, of course; and that is where Ridley Scott chose to site his filmic début: *The Duellists*.[13]

Yet, both gladiators and bullfighters are moved by the pursuit of honor, to be conquered by pleasing an audience in the enactment of a ritual. For bullfighting is not a game—the bull cannot win; he will be butchered one way or another. It is not a competitive sport, either, for there is no competition. Nor is bullfighting a theatrical event, for no reality is being represented there. This leaves us with bullfighting as a ritual, but how accessible is the ritual to the populace, if to view it one must pay for tickets as expensive as those required to attend an opera?

Indeed, bullfighting is a business, too. It can be simplified, but in its full splendor, bullfighting involves stadiums, rearing of a fighting lineage of bulls, trainers, trained horses, tailors, hordes of aspiring bullfighters, medics specialized in goring by horns, and even a specialized press, which in Spain may involve more than one nationwide periodical and at least a full-page story in any major newspaper. Small business it is not, and the size of the industry testifies to its significance, which, with variations, embraces all the Iberian peninsula (except Galicia and Northern Portugal), most of Southern France, and many New World countries, where the aficionado is significant.[14]

[12] Conrad (1908).

[13] Scott (1977).

[14] Barton (1989); Douglass (1997).

Bullfighting was practiced widely in Latin America; for example, in Uruguay where a Plaza de Toros remains in Colonia. But the wars of independence entailed rejecting much of what was seen as Spanish, such as its bullfighting. However, many of the attitudes and values that characterize bullfighting remained.

Wherever bullfighting is practiced, following anthropologist Julian Pitt-Rivers, one can read many meanings into the ritual's reenactment. However, one meaning that associates genders with the players in the bullfighting ritual has been around for some time, of course prior to Pitt-Rivers, and has been recalled over and over again is Carrie Douglass's *Toro muerto, vaca es: An Interpretation of the Spanish Bullfight.*[15] In this work, the Spanish woman bestows honor to her man inasmuch as she remains penetrated only by him, thus avoiding shame to befall on her man. Initially the woman's father is her guardian, who leads her as a virgin to her husband and thus retains his parental honor; and then her husband is her guardian, keeping his own honor as long as she remains faithful to him.[16] In this tradition men cannot acquire honor through their women, they can only hope not to lose it. Thus we have the saying regarding the (man's) idea of a woman's safety: *mujer honrada, en casa y con la pierna quebrada* (an honorable woman, at home with a broken leg).[17]

Male ambivalence toward females, expressed in the Madonna-whore dichotomy, may have its origin in the long and intense mother-son bond and relatively absent fathers. This may lead to the child splitting the image of the "devouring' mother and the nurturing one.

Additionally, in the preceding analysis, much is being made of the underlying role of women in bullfighting, even though they are completely absent in it.[18] Perhaps the role of women is

[15] Douglass (1984).

[16] A similar attitude can be found in song X—"Por culpa de una mujer" (Hernández, 1983).

[17] (Douglass, 1984, 248). Or in Hernández (1983, stanza 323): "Las mujeres, dende entonces,/ conocí a todas en una;/ya no he de probar fortuna/ con carta tan conocida: mujer y perra parida,/¡no se me acerca ninguna!"

[18] Though not from the arena. See the story of Conchita Cintron (Halton, 2009).

indeed exaggerated, but this dynamic relationship seems to be so pervasive in the Mediterranean that it deserves attention. Not only in Spain, but throughout the Mediterranean there is a strong, ambivalent and even contradictory stance of men toward women. This has been picked up by scholars, who found a pan-Mediterranean attitude toward honor-shame associated with the role of women in men's social standing, of the sort summarized here.[19] That male ambivalence toward females, expressed in the Madonna-whore dichotomy, may have its origin in the long and intense mother-son bond and relatively absent fathers. This may lead to the child splitting the image of the "devouring" mother and the nurturing one.[20] Anthropologist David Gilmore goes on to argue that, while such feelings may explain the origin of the Madonna-whore dichotomy, the ensuing ambivalence finds an expression in Andalusian song and poetry, which depict men as helpless, childlike, and dependent on women, while women are shown to be powerful and controlling.[21]

> In Portuguese bars, masculinity is expressed not in absolute terms but as relative to the other, and mostly by attempts to feminize the other through sexual innuendos or fondling his private parts. Physical expression of masculinity is reserved, in teamwork, for the garriadas.

One can apply this metaphor to bullfighting in that the bulls' owners offer guarantees that their bulls have never been "run." In that case, they could be considered virgins guarded by their ranchers. At the arena, they must be "controlled" by the matador who will ultimately defile the bull, drawing blood from him, but will be ennobled by the act only if it is done honorably; that is, according to the script. Then the audience can grant additional *honores* to the bullfighter, in the form of allowing him to take one or more of the bull's ears, plus his tail, or perhaps to encircle the arena to receive the standing ovation of the audience. That honor can also be bestowed on a bull, even when dead, if it has highly displayed the qualities expected of a fighting

[19] Schneider (1971); Saunders (1981); Gilmore (1982).

[20] Saunders (1981, 457).

[21] Gilmore (1982, 230).

bull; for, whether by the bull or the matador, honorable fighting is praised by the audience, as it was once praised by audiences of gladiator fights.

There are two types of *honores.* There is the personal honor, mostly associated with the care dedicated to the family and in particular to the women within it. That honor can only be lost. Then there is the other honor, which can be earned and which is the one that grants precedence when achieved through social recognition. At the bullfight, that recognition is secured by the bullfighter in elegantly putting his life at risk—particularly where it is most precious—according to the script. When well done, the bullfighter earns respect, yet even that respect, or honor, may be gradated, according to the "prizes," such as the bull's ears or the triumphant parade the bullfighter may be granted by the audience.

As in Spain, bullfighting in Portugal is a summer ritual, and something that men will brag about in bars when idle, like at Pardais, as per the account of Miguel Vale de Almeida. Commensality at bars is far from random. Men drink together and take turns paying for others' drinks. Foreigners cannot expect drinks to be paid for. Drinking involves talking, mostly bragging and exaggerating about hunting deals, but masculinity-related prowess is always prominent, from manly postures to seduction stories, though rarely through physical violence, as is more frequently the case in Anglo-Saxon and German bar brawls. In a Portuguese bar, Vale de Almeida argues, masculinity is expressed not in absolute terms but relative to the other, and mostly by attempts to feminize the other through sexual innuendos or fondling his private parts. Physical expression of masculinity is reserved, in teamwork, for the *garriadas.*[22]

Bullfighting in Southern Portugal is different. The bull is not killed, and the ritual is more of an equestrian adventure. But the lower-class *garriadas'* approach Spanish bullfighting is as a sport in which the bull also is not killed and there is more teamwork. The team leader defies a young bull while half a dozen teammates back him up in a straight line between him and the bull. The team leader must jump over the charging bull's horns and secure

[22] Almeida (1996, 90–91).

himself to the beast by grabbing the beast's neck while the rest of his team grabs the beast by whatever they can with the purpose of immobilizing it.

Like the Portuguese, the Catalonians have merchant orientations, which make them a more practical people, little interested in death. Merchants lack the morbidity that gives place to the poetry of bullfighting.[23] Perhaps this is why bullfighting was banned in Catalonia. We will see more of this in Panama.

Many do not see the ritual in bullfighting and prefer to focus on the result of the performance—a dead bull skillfully dealt with by a team bound to a rigid apprentice system—reducing the process to mere folk craft.[24] Nonetheless, reducing bullfighting to its coda, a dead bull, and missing the ritual that brought about the symphony, is like attempting to read the significance of a birthday party only through the remains of the cake; some light will be shed, but it will not be very illuminating.

Bullfighting made it to the New World through the Spanish settlers and is still practiced today in the most traditionally Spanish of the former colonies, those with shores along the Pacific: México, Colombia, Perú, and Ecuador, and also in Venezuela. There may also be garriadas or other forms in countries like Costa Rica, in addition to the *vaquejadas* in Brazil.

In Caracas, when the Nuevo Circo arena was opened in 1919, it was large enough to accommodate a tenth of the city's population. Gómez was President; he was more passionate for cockfighting, but we turn to him later. For now it suffices to call our attention to what Latin American ritual audiences admire, for it might be what they admire in a fighting leader as well.

[23] Regarding the commercial oriented Catalans Hemingway wrote "With them [Catalans], as in Galicia, life is too practical for there to be much of the hardest kind of common sense nor much feeling about death" (Hemingway, 1932, 132).

[24] Mitchell (1986).

# 8

# In Venezuela, Fierro and Sombra Assess the Marcha Restauradora

"Right, Sombra, tell me, who runs this place?"

"Gómez does. Juan Vicente Gómez. A very interesting character, Fierro. He has run this place for about four decades."[1]

"Long. He must have been good with the facón."

"With the machete, he was, yes, but not only, Fierro; he was a cunning leader, too."

"Tell me more, Sombra, the distilled Gómez, the rum of him."

"Like with cats, there are many ways to skin Venezuelans. One way renders them into Andinos or not."

"Andinos like from the mountains, Sombra?"

"Precisely, men from the Andes, as opposed to those of the lowlands, are more reserved, more tradition oriented, more ritualistic, and more respectful of authority and are a population whose elite is mostly comprised of landowners and clergy. In Gómez's particular case, even more so. He came from Táchira, so far away, so close to Colombia, that it was mostly left alone. People made their living off the land, mostly on cattle, no slaves nor latifundia; poor schooling, too. In being traditional they were also finicky guardians of loyalty."

"So, Sombra? What is wrong with that?"

"Nothing, Fierro, but knowing that helps to understand Gómez. In being a farmer of his family's land for almost a century,

[1] For a documentary of Juan Vicente Gómez in Youtube.com, see http://bit.ly/5hpBSF. Accessed January 2, 2017.

he learned of the responsibility that goes with it. He learned management tools there and then, and not much more because his father died early and he had to take over the family business."

"Not a bad school at all, Sombra!"

"Indeed, Fierro, but those were times of duress and threats. Not surprisingly, he believed that punishment kept people's minds focused on getting on with their duties."

"Nothing wrong with that either, Sombra!"

"Yes, all this is very basic, Fierro. At the farm, Gómez also developed a keen understanding of how to make sure orders were carried out. He would wake earlier than his men, while it was still dark, and survey progress with his own eyes and provide feedback a few hours later. The sun had been up a long time when he would have an Andino breakfast that would keep him for most of the rest of the day, throughout his life, as the belief in the elevating power of hard work and punishment would, too."

"A bit like Rosas, Sombra."

"Indeed, Fierro, except that Gómez did not distrust educated people. He also showed his respect for discipline, order, reliability and cleanliness—virtues he appreciated among the German traders at nearby Cúcuta, Colombia or at San Cristóbal in Venezuela. That is how far Gómez's land was from the Oriental Caracas."

"Clever of him, Sombra!"

"Yes, Fierro. Gómez learned to work and produce handsome profits that he shared with his family while observing a reserved relationship with his neighbors."

"Forget the neighbors, Sombra!"

"No, Fierro, because it was at the farm that Gómez learned to keep the neighbors neither too far nor too close, just at the right distance, a principle, that like his diet he would practice as president, in both internal and international affairs. That's how he kept the clergy off the state and kept Venezuela neutral in World War I."

"Clever of him!"

> "Cipriano Castro's is not an army. They have ranks and war bills, but the so-called soldiers are all young peasants, related to each other by blood or marriage, each fighting their own war. Were it not for Gómez's strong disciplinary punishments, they would have disbanded early. But when they obeyed they did by and large for allegiance. They know each other well. They know their families, too. They know well what to expect from each other. Any lies are short lived there."

"Precisely, Fierro. He would apply the same principle when president of Venezuela. While not exactly neighbors, American oil prospectors earned much support from Gómez, who nonetheless refused US pressures to enter World War I, which in any case, Gómez believed would be won by the Germans."

Fierro was assessing the land from Spinoza's back, idly listening to Sombra's musings, who continued:

"Simple and fine he was, Fierro, until he was forty years old. He would have remained a farmer all his life, enjoying the festivities and bullfights at Tariba in August, were it not for his comrade Cipriano Castro, far more educated than Gómez was; also vainer and vulnerable."

"What do you mean by that, Sombra?"

"Gómez was a young man when he met Castro, who dreamed of taking over Caracas, which was made to sound like it was ten times the size of Cúcuta, and better."

"Caracas sounds like a fun town; continue, Sombra!"

"In 1886, Gómez's compadre, Evaristo Jaime, fell serving under Castro. Shared sorrow would bring these strange bedfellows ever closer, and Castro would later become godfather to Gómez's first son.[2] By 1892, Gómez had joined Castro's drive on Caracas. They lost and spent six years exiled in Colombia; not far from Gómez's own farm, but still, in exile."

"It goes with being brave, Sombra! There is a price!"

"And sometimes a reward, Fierro. In 1899, Gómez, with Castro, crossed the river back into Venezuela. Gómez now had the rank of General and was second in command with a managerial function: to take care of logistics and monitor the cost of supplies, which would be paid for once they took over Caracas."

"That's some faith in a cause, Sombra!" said Fierro sardonically while caressing his long whiskers, adding, mockingly, "Those traders must have believed in Castro's cause, Sombra!"

"It is more likely that the donors had no alternative, Fierro," Sombra conceded, while, like Fierro, he cast his eyes on the high altitude plateau."

Sombra continued, "Castro's is not an army. They have ranks and war bills, but the so-called soldiers are all young peasants, related to each other by blood or marriage, each fighting their

[2] On the strangeness of the dyad Castro-Gómez, see Vazquez (2008).

own war. Were it not for Gómez's strong disciplinary punishments, they would have disbanded early. But when they obeyed they did so mostly for allegiance. The soldiers know each other well. They know their families, too. They know well what to expect from each other. Any lies are short lived there."

"It reminds me of a montonera, Sombra!"

"In many ways it is a montonera, Fierro, but the leaders have endured six years in exile. That's too long a wait for a montonera. These people have a cause, Fierro! Even women joined in, some are the officers' lovers and others have no fixed man, though they have their preferences. But all have collective functions, too, some washing, others cooking. They are in war, but it is a fighting family."

"That does not sound like a montonera, Sombra! Montoneras are like thunderous lightening! They attack and disband."

"Precisely, Fierro! These are people at war! Some will die and it will mean a family's mourning. A brave man by the name of Régulo Olivares will suffer a bad machete blow to his face. It will be so bad that nobody will expect him to survive it. Olivares survived the blow, but he carried the scar on his face for the rest of his life."

"That's the price of courage, Sombra! If there were no price, all would be brave!"

"Indeed, Fierro. These brave men were fortunate. Except for the battle of Tocuyito, they did not face many occasions to put their courage to the test. The government's regular armies would disband upon facing Castro's ragtime army, leaving their weapons and

> "One chief cannot be everywhere at the same time, he will have to delegate his grand strategy to smaller chiefs, whom he will have to trust to carry out his orders or adapt them as best they can where they need to be deployed. Those smaller chiefs will need to be respected by their followers, whose ultimate allegiance lies with the big chief, but who know that in following their small chief they will be fulfilling the big chief's will. The small chiefs, Fierro, are unlikely to muster the wherewithal they need to lead their followers if the big chief has broken their backs, particularly if done so in front of his other followers. So, if the big chief wants his orders to be carried out he will need the effective collaboration of proud, smaller chiefs, themselves capable of leading."

ammunition behind. When they fought they had too many generals to fight for; disunited they could not win."[3]

"Of course they could not win, Sombra! There can only be one big chief! There are lots of smaller chiefs, but only one can be chief of them all!"

"Indeed, Fierro, that is what Gómez would always say. They had only one chief and all knew the chief was Cipriano Castro, who was small and not particularly wealthy. But he had schooling and was also a brave man. That is why he was a chief."

"Leadership, Sombra, has not to do with size, or schooling! Courage is paramount. Men need to know their leaders have balls! Put that in doubt and the would-be followers will find better things to do on their own!"

"Balls may not be the only thing, Fierro, but Gómez argued that he learned with Castro to tell the difference between officers and a chief. They had many officers in their army, but few who had the stuff to become chiefs."

"Usually there is only one man left standing, Sombra! The rest will put their tails between their legs."

"Perhaps, Fierro, but the best leader will not pressure them up to the point of their humiliation."

"Why not, Sombra? What's wrong in clearly showing who is in command?"

"Fierro, a large organization, like an army, must have one sole chief, but cannot be run without hundreds of loyal sub-chiefs, if you understand what I mean."

Gómez would praise his subordinates in public and reprimand them only in private. It would take a few decades until this basic maxim would make it to management textbooks. Gómez would remove his subordinates if he felt they failed to exercise the leadership qualities that their rank required.

"Speak out, Sombra!"

"One chief cannot be everywhere at the same time, he will have to delegate his grand strategy to smaller chiefs, whom he will have to trust to carry out his orders or adapt them as best they can where they need to be deployed."

[3] Regular army General Andrade would divide his own subordinates like Generals Ferrer and Fernández who would not communicate their individual plans and ended up exposing their men to friendly fire (Velásquez, 1978, 133).

"So?"

"Fierro, those smaller chiefs will need to be respected by their followers, whose ultimate allegiance lies with the big chief, but who know that in following their small chief they will be fulfilling the big chief's will."

"So, Sombra?"

"The small chiefs, Fierro, are unlikely to muster the wherewithal they need to lead their followers if the big chief has broken their backs, particularly if in front of his followers. So, if the big chief wants his orders to be carried out he will need the effective collaboration of proud, smaller chiefs, themselves capable of leading."

"Cipriano Castro knew that there were those who had rank but no guts, those who would betray their chiefs, like they betrayed the generals of the regular army as the Andinos made their advance. The regulars were afraid to lose and have their lives go to waste. They preferred to change sides and join Castro. By accepting the offers of acquiescence of the cowardly traitors, Castro weakened the regular army and paved his way to a swift victory. In any case, the traitors had chosen to turn into zombies."

"Be practical, Sombra! How did Gómez confer authority without undermining his own?"[4]

"Now, this basic premise of managerial effectiveness is all too frequently overlooked in managerial practice."

"Fine with praising subordinates in public, but they cannot be led to believe that they are good enough to replace the big chief when he is not ready to go yet!"

"That is the art of leadership, Fierro! I am glad you are not as thick as you sometimes sound!"

"Watch it, Sombra!"

"But you are right, Fierro, in that some men's effectiveness will be limited to carry out orders, while others have what is required to be leaders. Cipriano Castro knew that only too well, and he used people. He knew there were those who had rank but no guts, those who would betray their chiefs, like they betrayed the generals of the regular army as the Andinos made their advance. The

[4] Velásquez, op. cit. 355 and 356.

regulars were afraid to lose and have their lives go to waste. They preferred to change sides and join Castro."[5]

"Cowards, Sombra! Castro should have killed them on the spot!"

"Fierro, those without a cause, he would manage with a bag of gold coins in one hand and a whip in the other, thus preceding the motivational paradigm in managerial textbooks by decades.[6] Had he killed them on the spot, their followers would have been set loose, and that would have only prolonged a war Castro might not have won, Fierro. By accepting the offers of the cowardly traitors, Castro weakened the regular army and paved his way to a swift victory. The traitors in any case had chosen to turn into zombies."

"So, Castro took Caracas with Gómez; what next, Sombra?"

"Well, do you remember that Castro was vain? After a few years he surrendered."

> "Cipriano Castro fell ill and trusted no one. Once he was being operated upon, or should have had an operation. Castro was slit open, but then an aide-de-camp present in the surgical room pulled a revolver and stuck it up the belly of the surgeon, warning him that he would be a dead man if anything happened to Castro. The surgeon pretended he had 'fixed' the chief and sewed him up again! Castro emerged alive and so did his surgeon. That's why Castro had to have a second operation, a year later, this time in Berlin. No one would dare tackle Castro's health needs in Caracas anymore!"

[5] After the battle of Tocuyito, Castro and Gómez had less than 1,500 men with them, while the regular army had more than five times that, in addition to being closer to supplies in Caracas, and being better armed too. However, they were disunited, and the regular army sought an armistice. Castro requested that General Andrade surrender. In less than a month, General Andrade had resigned and Castro was president of Venezuela (Velásquez, 1978,182–83).

[6] "For many managers, motivation and manipulation mean one and the same thing; but employees know the difference" (Levinson, 1973, 70). Velásquez, 1978, 356. In fact, although the carrot-and-stick idiom as an incentive-punishment dyad was probably used earlier in management, the earliest reference of this expression in the *Supplement* to the *Oxford English Dictionary* is to *The Economist* magazine in the December 11, 1948, issue. However, in that magazine the earliest expression is in the June 29, 1946, issue, p. 1033, with a discussion on human nature regarding work that spills onto p. 1034.

"What do you mean, he surrendered, Sombra? He was brave, he cannot have caved in!"

"Well, he did, to flattery and vice, he did, Fierro!"

"Oh, no!"

"Perhaps he was too small to feel attractive and take the initiative to flirt with women, but he would accept girlish virgins dressed as schoolgirls, fetched for him by his flatterers."

"Sick, Sombra!"

"Very much so, Fierro! As corruption and vengeance festered, the loyal Gómez chose to keep a distance, but that only fueled suspicion and intrigue. Particularly when Cipriano Castro fell ill and would trust no one once he was undergoing—or should have been undergoing—surgery."

"What do you mean, they did not operate him?"

"Fierro, they did! Sort of. Castro was slit open, but then an aide-de-camp present in the surgical room pulled a revolver and stuck it up the belly of the surgeon, warning him that he would be a dead man if anything happened to Castro."

"It should have been a facón, Sombra!"

> "Taming a people through torture, exile and imprisonment for decades is the way forward? Is it the right price to pay for progress? Of course not! Though I often wonder whether the people Gómez put out were any better than himself only because they opposed him.
>
> "Toward his end, Gómez in official uniform looked very much like some tin-pot tropical Kaiser, far different from the man who spent six years in exile to fight his way back into Caracas all the way from Táchira."

"Too close to the United States for that, Fierro, it was a revolver!"

"What next, Sombra?"

"The surgeon pretended he had 'fixed' the chief and sewed him up again! Castro emerged alive and so did his surgeon. That's why Castro had to have a second operation, a year later, this time in Berlin. No one would dare tackle his health needs in Caracas anymore!"

"Amazing story, Sombra! That is the expression of lack of trust: nobody around to risk his life for you!"

"Well, Fierro, you cannot just win a war. The real challenge is what you do with it later."

"So, what next, Sombra!"

"A few years later Castro was only a scarecrow of what he had been, he had earned the enmity of just about all foreigners, and Gómez took over. Castro remained in exile in Puerto Rico—close but not too close, as Gómez had learned to manage his neighbors."

"So, despite all his professed loyalty, Gómez in fact did Castro in!"

"I guess it boils down to that, yes, Fierro. But you see, perhaps Gómez judged that his loyalty to Venezuela came first."

"Only valid if Castro was against Venezuela, Sombra!"

"Well, perhaps he was, Fierro, in the sense that he was no longer fit to govern Venezuela."

"Or was he unfit to hold his ground, Sombra? Like in a facón duel?"

"Nor precisely, Fierro."

"Ah, I see, Castro was unable to hold his ground in a land of intrigues."

"Can we agree that perhaps Castro had become more of a nuisance than helpful, Fierro?"

"Nuisance to whom, Sombra? To Venezuelans or to the Neapolitans?"

"Put it this way, Fierro, Castro had defied Venezuela's closest commercial allies; it was bad for business and the creditors' navies had besieged Venezuela's ports."[7]

"I am not concerned with business, Sombra, but with honor!"

"When business is poor, Fierro, honor becomes tradable!"

"Gómez quieted people with commercial concessions; his opponents were systematically appeased with opportunities, rights to auction cattle, concessions on oil fields, to sell alcoholic beverages, granting monopoly rights over salt and tobacco, and more. He learned that with Cipriano Castro after the battle of Tocuyito, when Castro bought out the government officers that wanted to hold on to their privileges after a takeover of the country by Castro."

[7] In chapter 12 of "Gómez, un enigma histórico," Jorge Olavarría (2007) argues that the sidelining of Castro was not arranged by Gómez when under foreign pressure.

Fierro crossed himself. "Good gracious! I never thought I would hear another gaucho say that, Sombra!" Spinoza raises in his hind legs and neighs, "*Et non tantum mortis damnetur.*"[8]

"Hold it, Fierro! Condemn me not yet! What if people become unemployed and their families hungry on account of your unyielding penchant for honor?"

"Dishonor is worse than death, Sombra! You are proposing to stick to a life not worth living!"

"So, you would rather die honorably than seek a better opportunity to have it your way?"

"You got me there, Sombra! I had agreed with Artigas earlier, hadn't I?"

"You did, Fierro!"

"Then, only for the sake of consistency, I will hold Spinoza for now."

"I am not sure you will like what comes next, Fierro. In any case, Gómez in power lavishly 'greased' all his enemies' hands, and that was it. That's economic change management for you, Fierro!"

"What do you mean, Sombra?"

"Gómez quieted people down with commercial concessions; his opponents were systematically appeased with opportunities, rights to auction cattle, concessions on oil fields, licenses to sell alcoholic beverages, monopoly rights over salt and tobacco, and more. He learned that with Castro after the battle of Tocuyito, when he bought out the government officers who wanted to hold on to their privileges after a takeover by Castro."

"What about those who would not sell themselves out, Sombra?"

"They would be exiled, imprisoned and tortured or face forced labor, Fierro."

"Sombra, tell me the truth, what was good about Gómez?"

"Peace, if you think it was worth it, Fierro."

"Peace at the expense of what, Sombra, of a generalized lack of principles? You will also find peace at the cemeteries, Sombra!"

8 "Death is not enough," Spinoza (1667, chapter 8, paragraph 25). Translated by Gossett (1883).

"Fierro, peace enabled the almost one thousand-mile road built to connect Caracas with Táchira. Peace brought all the feeder roads that sprang out of the Táchira-Caracas road and helped integrate a country that only vaguely existed prior to Gómez. Peace enabled the upgrading of the sanitation standards of Venezuela. After that came the European immigrants who injected the skills that were scarce and the foreign investment that found oil in Venezuela.[9] Would Gómez have done better not allowing foreign corporations to prospect for oil and instead sit on it without even knowing where he was sitting?"

Recruitment under Gómez was based geographically. It started with people from Táchira and Venezuela continued to be run by Andinos for almost half a century!

"But, Sombra, are you arguing that taming a people through torture, exile and imprisonment for decades is the way forward? Is it the right price to pay for progress?"

"Of course not, Fierro, though I often wonder whether the people he put out were any better than him, just because they opposed him. But fair enough, Fierro. I guess you are right. Toward his end, Gómez in official uniform looked very much like some tin-pot tropical Kaiser, far from the man who spent six years in exile to fight his way back into Caracas all the way from Táchira."

"A sad end for a once brave and righteous man, Sombra!"

"True, Fierro. But see how he stuck to his early farm-life imprints, including respect for Teutonic traders and their outfits."

"So what, Sombra?"

"So? Gómez was a responsible creature who grew up in a land where there was not much to emulate, except the German immigrants. He chose his beacons well. Táchira's Teutons were not only tidy and hardworking, they were entrepreneurial as well."

"Like when?"

Loyalty and the high performing teamwork it brings with it, is more readily achieved in Latin America by bringing together people who already know each other very well.

[9] Personal communication with Ramón J. Veláquez, December, 5, 2009.

"Like when they kicked off the first commercial airline in the Americas, Fierro, second in the whole planet!"

"Did they?"

"Yes they did, out of Gómez's region, too, and it was run with German Junkers planes. Gómez respected hard work and focus. That's positive, Fierro, is it not?"[10]

"It depends on the purpose of prejudice and punishment, Sombra."

"Ah! Fierro! There goes the inflammable montonera leader again! I am right in doubting whether Gómez's opponents would have been better than himself!"

Fierro laughed Sombra off, who continued, "Fierro, Gómez respected industriousness. He understood that an idle army breeds trouble. He realized that too many officers yawning bored in forts is cause for trouble. Gómez was right in that he believed in peasant armies, soldiers with machetes, alert to the bouts of snakes and spiders, fighting the ever-encroaching forests. This is why Gómez would quell uprisings with commanders with no army function and with rural businesses of their own. Their peasants would know the land better than any army officer would.[11] Gómez believed in edifying work, this is why he had so many roads built, with people not machines, to employ people. When university students protested, he closed the university—for a decade, too—arguing that if the students did not want to study they should work! Even so, not all was negative about him, not even at the end, Fierro!"

Fierro shrugged his shoulders and pulled the reins of his horse, crying aloud, "Let's move on, Spinoza, I would rather trot over the perfidy of the swamps of Monay on our way to Central America than fathom what power does to the initially brave! Sombra, follow me, if you care!"

The non-Andinos are likely to take revenge. The people will have learned not so much to trust who you know but to distrust who you don't know. It will take Venezuelans a long time before they recover. Whether all the roads one can count on Gómez's favor were worth all the time under Gómez, is up to the Venezuelans to figure out.

[10] The German-Colombian Air Transport Company (Sociedad Colombo Alemana de Transporte Aéreo, Scadta) was constituted on December 5, 1919 and flew from Barranquilla to Puerto Colombia on a Junkers F13 (Banco de la República de Colombia) (Thomas, 2005, 978–79).

[11] Velásquez (1978, 352–53).

## Four Decades at the Helm: Lessons on Change Management, Recruitment and Motivation

"What can we say we learned here, Sombra?"

"Quite a lot, Fierro."

"Like what?"

"Fierro, in the first place, we confirmed what we had seen regarding recruitment and teamwork in the Brazilian Federalist Revolt with Gumercindo. In the second place, we saw how a leader may use a variety of motivational instruments to secure his goals. In the third place, we saw hints of how the first imprints on an uneducated leader may shape his future allegiances, like in Gomez's respect for all things German."

"Recruitment under Gómez was based geographically. It started with people from Táchira and Venezuela and continued to be run with Andinos for almost half a century!"

"Good for Andinos, Sombra, but what about the rest?"

"The rest plotted against Gomez constantly; almost twenty significant revolts were suppressed."

"It shows that they were not up to Andinos, Sombra. But is it fair to rule only with an 'in group'?"

"Not altogether fair, Fierro. But that is up to Venezuelans to sort out. I am concerned with organizational effectiveness, and the lesson I draw is rather obvious to me. But it needs to be repeated because it will be neglected by American Scientific Management."

"Why Sombra?"

"Only God knows why, Fierro, except that the alternative works for North Americans, who step in and out of romantic relationships with greater ease than we do.[12]"

"What does marriage have to do with work, Sombra!"

"Well, not all, but it is an indicator suggesting that North Americans can get along with each other well enough to cohabitate, knowing less of each other than other peoples do. This may also mean that they can form work teams more easily than people who need to know much more about each other."

[12] At least faster than romantic couples in Europe, Japan, Australian and New Zealand in *The State of Culture, Class and Family* (Hoschschild, 2009). Also see Cherlin (2009) where the author argues that America shows the highest rate of transitory relationships among advanced economies, updating earlier studies in Cherlin (1992, 70–71).

"Sombra, could this be why the U-Haul business model catering to individuals still has not caught on elsewhere as it did in North America, for this company founded in 1945 and with yearly revenues over $4 billion?"

"Perhaps, Fierro, North Americans move on much more frequently than other peoples. It is not surprising that they can fit into teams more quickly, too. They would not move so frequently if they could not fit into teams, would they?"

"Sombra, so much so that Americans seem to fit into romantic relationships faster, too."

"Yes, Fierro. Could it mean that Americans, in being more autonomous, need to know less about the other in order to feel comfortable?"

"Sombra, perhaps that is why American Scientific Management stresses hiring individuals from the market, because the individuals they find there work well together more quickly than ours would when fished out from different ponds."

"Precisely, Fierro. It might not sound like much, but that these people from Táchira would hold Venezuela for so long does have some meaning, doesn't it?"

"It sure does to me, Sombra, particularly if you consider that Montevideans, Gumercindo, Conselheiro and the Contestado people would recruit in the same way in Brazil."

"And the Rio de Janeiro samba schools do the same, too, Fierro!"

"Yes, there is some learning to be taken home, Sombra!"

"There is more to Gómez's leadership, Fierro."

Americans move on much more frequently than other peoples do. So much so that Americans seem to fit into romantic relationships faster too. This could mean that Americans, in being more autonomous, need to know less about the other in order to feel comfortable to work together. It should not come as a surprise that Americans can fit into teams more quickly too. Americans would not change cities so frequently if they could not fit into work teams; perhaps that is why American Scientific Management stresses hiring individuals from the market, because the individuals they find in the market work well together faster than ours would work among us when fished out of the larger pond in the same way. Gómez knew this well and recruited at Táchira.

"Yes, the motivational instruments, Sombra. Let us summarize them. Start with the carrot motivations, like in the metaphor, 'carrot and stick.' "

"I would not call all instruments motivational, Fierro. Some were destined to cement a developmental strategy through strategic alliances."

"Like which, Sombra?"

"Gómez built roads and other infrastructure with the support of cement and asphalt manufacturers. He also supported foreign oil prospectors when there was not much local knowledge on the subject."

"But how did he get the people to do what he wanted, Sombra?"

"At first there was a cause, remember? It was the Marcha Restauradora, during which Gómez learned there were high officers who could be bought off."

"Yes, skunks, Sombra! All of them, skunks! What about the rest, afterwards?"

"Gómez bought them off, too. He gave them concessions, like rights to hold auctions, to sell cattle and the like."

"That was the carrot side of his instruments, Sombra. But don't forget the political prisoners!"

"True, that was the stick side of his policy. He fiercely punished his opponents with exile, imprisonment, forced labor and torture."

"There is no greatness in belittling great men! Gómez believed the Germans played fair in business and deserved what they achieved through their hard work. That is why he hired a Prussian-trained Chilean officer to found the Venezuelan Military Academy. Perhaps that is why he ended up his life dressed like a Kaiser. In a way, his appreciation of the German work ethos became his own when governing Venezuela."

"Occasionally death, too, Sombra?"

"It would not surprise me, Fierro. But by buying some off he managed to avoid excessive punishing."

"Did he do the killing himself, face to face, with a facón, as in a duel?"

"No, Fierro. He must have had them killed."

"A coward then, Sombra."

"Perhaps, but there is no record of anyone daring to call him that to his face, Fierro!"

"And what would you say of his upbringing, Sombra?"

"Founded on discipline, Fierro. He was frugal, orderly and respectful of hard work. That is what Cipriano Castro saw in him: a reliable collaborator; like one capable of keeping tabs of who had paid for the Marcha Restauradora, for example."

"One who admired foreigners, too, Sombra!"

"Not all foreigners, Fierro. He particularly admired Germans."

"Why, Sombra? Because they were the first thing he saw?"

"Don't be silly, Fierro. There is no greatness in belittling great men! Gómez believed the Germans played fair in business and deserved what they achieved through their hard work. That is why he hired a Prussian-trained Chilean officer to found the Venezuelan Military Academy. Perhaps that is why he ended up his life dressed like a Kaiser. In a way, his appreciation of the German work ethos became his own when governing Venezuela. Besides, Fierro, with the tax revenues he paid off the foreign debt because he believed in feeling better owing to no one. He paid the domestic debt holders and the foreign ones."

"He loved the Germans so much he ended up dressed like one, Sombra!"

"He cannot have been a very inventive man, and ended up looking like a bit of a fool. You are right, Fierro! Still, it's over."

"It never is, Sombra. The non-Andinos are likely to take revenge; the people will have learned not so much to trust who you know but to distrust who you don't know. It will take Venezuelans a long time before they recover. All the roads you count in his favor will not have been worth all the time under Gómez."

"Still, Fierro, it is up to the Venezuelans to figure that one out."

# 9

# Panama Secedes from Colombia, and Fierro Looks for Heroism in Costa Rica

> "Perhaps Colombians should have foreseen the outcome of staffing a fragile and coveted spot with a weak personality. But they did not, or saw the risk but did nothing. Inaction is quite common among poor managers. It is as if they hoped for the best."

Hard as they are to come by, heroes are quite abundant. Their opposites ought to be more so, but seldom does history register their treacherous achievements, except when they succeed, like in the case of Panama."

"The non-heroes are fit for the facón, Sombra, to make kebabs out of them. That's all. Who dares ask what the kebab is made with?"

"Precisely, Fierro, this is why the case of Colombian Colonel Eliseo Torres Gutiérrez is so interesting, because those who fail to rise to heroism when expected to will be forever scorned."[1]

"Tell me more, Sombra, but do not mention his name again."

"All right, Fierro, 'this person' is depicted by fellow Colombians as a Colombian who had sought a military life for himself, not for any particular love for the martial arts, least of all to serve his country, but simply to make a decent living."

[1] This is a personal rendition of historical data as reported in several sources, such as Diaz Espino (2004), and the one by Lemaitre Román (1980) or its 2003 reprint. Many related accounts can also be read at the Cultural Department of Colombia's Banco de la República: www.banrepcultural.org.

"A skunk like so many I met at the frontier, Sombra."

"Whatever, Fierro, he is depicted as not particularly bright, perhaps obedient but lacking in initiative and inclined to hit the bottle. Unfortunately for Colombia and perhaps even for Panama, this man was Colombia's point man in the coastal city of Colón, on November 3, 1904."

"Wrong man at the wrong time and place, Sombra. How did the Colombians fall for that?"

"Well that is an important managerial lesson, is it not, Fierro? Perhaps Colombians should have foreseen the outcome of staffing a fragile and coveted spot with a weak personality. But they did not, or perhaps they saw the risk but did nothing. Inaction is quite common among poor managers. It is as if they hoped for the best."

> If those who fail, and those who appoint those who fail, knew that the facón waited for them, they would not accept those appointments nor would they be promoted to them.

"Cut it short! How did matters evolve, Sombra?"

"All right, Fierro. There and then, through this man with a brain the size of a bird, Colombia would have had a chance to foil the independence of Panama, which was being midwifed by US money and gunboats. Colombian officers entrusted with suppressing the conspiracy were arrested by mercenaries upon arrival at Panama City."

"Poor Colombians, Sombra!"

"Not yet, Fierro. When this man was informed of the situation at the appropriate setting, the bar of a hotel in Colón, he is said to have burst into irate expletives and demanded the immediate release of his superiors, preventively jailed by a secessionist Panamanian faction backed by a treacherous Colombian army officer in Panama City."

"Well, there was some manhood left in him after all, Sombra!"

"At least he played by the script, Fierro. He even issued an ultimatum; he wanted his orders carried out 'by two p.m.!' Or else he would order fire upon any Americans on the street."

"Not bad, Sombra, not bad at all!"

"Well, Fierro, it is easy to bark inside the hotel bar, or even—through his Police Chief—at the lonely US consul in Colón, Mr. Malmrose."

"How did the consul take it, Sombra?"

"Well, he did something about it. Preventively, the US gunboat *Nashville* disembarked forty-two armed men to protect American lives around the train station, which was turned into a safe haven. Americans were ordered to shoot back only if shot at first."

Colombians believe that had this man fired at least a single shot to defend Colombian soil; that shot could have made the difference between ignominy and martyrdom. Panama's secession was not one can call edifying for future generations. When treason goes unpunished, its outcome breeds contempt, distrust; and undermines all what one would want to stand for.

"Did the Colombian officer live up to his historical mandate, Sombra?"

"Well, Fierro, at first it seemed like he would. During close to ninety minutes, Colombian soldiers appeared to be inclined to make good their chief's ultimatum, but nothing happened."

"What happened next, Sombra! Be quick!"

"Nothing, Fierro. That is, Panama became independent. Colombia lost!"

"What do you mean, Sombra? This is not a soccer match, for God's sake! What happened?"

"Well, that is what happened, Fierro. You wanted a short story, this is it! Colombians believe that had this man fired at least a single shot, that shot could have made the difference between ignominy and martyrdom."

"Of course, Sombra! He should have charged, too!"

"But you see, Fierro, the man was only a poor fool leading under the influence of alcohol. One can only attempt to explain what might have passed through his mind at the time."

"He simply chickened out, Sombra, that's all!"

"To be fair, there were civilians at the train station; perhaps he had a heart after all. Also, he may have wondered whether the *Nashville* gunboat had called for reinforcements; he may have weighed his actions against that, including that the only Colombian gunboat in place chose to sail into the Caribbean."

"Weigh what you wish, Sombra! But the outcome is what counts; he handed over his sacred soil without a fight! Only cowards do that!"

"I guess that is a fair rendition, Fierro. The fact is that this man retreated, Panama became independent, and the Americans built the Canal, which, much to Panama's chagrin, remained in US possession for almost a century."

General Huertas López was only 26 years old and was ambitious, he already had a Panamanian family and seditious Panamanians offered him a high position in the Republic-to-be. General Huertas López certainly had no scruples and perhaps there were no limits to his treachery. Had he been French, in France he could perhaps have aspired to be a Talleyrand, and he would have, like Tallyerand, taken colossal bribes for the setting of new frontiers; which is what Huertas López did in Panama. But because he was in Panama, not in France, he is remembered abroad for having been a crook. In Panama he is a hero and has a footpath over Las Bovedas named after him, in the *Casco Viejo* of Panama city.

"Did this person face a Colombian firing squadron, Sombra?"

"Apparently not, Fierro. This man subsequently took residence in Cartagena, Colombia, where he took a series of low-key positions in what altogether amounted to an uneventful life. He could have been a hero, but he chose not to."

"Despicable behavior, Sombra!"

"Well, we do not know all the facts, Fierro. But if they were anything like what we believe happened, the outcome was not one can call edifying for future generations. When that behavior goes unpunished, it breeds contempt, distrust; it undermines all that one would want to stand for."

"Indeed it did, Sombra. I do not want to hear that coward's name again!"

"Don't rush, Fierro, we do not know all the circumstances. The man was depicted as a drunkard, he should never have been allocated to a position of such responsibility. But there again, we also know that the American President Nixon hit the bottle more frequently that he should, and his responsibilities at the time were much more serious.[2] The issue is why and how people unfit for the job are entrusted with its execution. Once they fail, it is easy to put all the blame on them, But how could that happen, Fierro?"

[2] Hitchens (2001, 134).

> "Even a traffic policeman would not agree to be deprived of his whistle! Why did Colombian army officers agree to be separated from their armed soldiers? The fact is that upon arrival in Panama, the Colombian officers were arrested by General Huertas López, a Colombian who had changed sides. Another traitor!"

"Because earlier cowards like them were not put before a firing squad when they failed, Sombra! That's how!"

"What about those who appointed them, Fierro?"

"Sombra, come here," says Fierro as he unsheathes his facón. "See this?" he says, as he walks toward Sombra."

"It is hard not to see it, Fierro, put it away."

"Sombra, this is the point of the facón. If those who fail, and those who appoint those who fail, knew that the facón waited for them, they would not accept those appointments nor would they be promoted to them. It is quite simple, Sombra, don't glorify!"

"Perhaps, Fierro, but before they fail, one cannot be sure that the circumstances will in fact be beyond their capabilities. In appointing them to what eventually becomes an exceedingly challenging ordeal, there was an act of faith, Fierro. Perhaps it was even well intentioned, in the sense that exposure to challenges develops people."

"An act of faith? My foot, Sombra! Those entrusted with no less than the defense of the soil, or the business their children will live on cannot afford acts of faith! What I am saying, Sombra, is that the facón clears people's minds, that's all. If they know there is a facón waiting for them, they will stay focused and behave."

"It is not hard to see your point, Fierro. But why do you think a fiasco happened precisely there?"

"Sombra, the man earned a salary for doing nothing; that is not good for manhood. He got used to doing nothing, and nothing he did when it was expected of him to put his life at stake."

"True, Fierro, but where is your capacity for empathy? Put yourself in this man's shoes for a minute. Panama was coming out of a long internecine war. Colombia, probably made aware of the possibility of a seditious movement in Panama, sends fresh troops, almost five hundred of them, through Colón, and under new leadership because they did not trust their General in command in Panama City, General Huertas Lopez."

"So, Sombra, move on!"

"Fierro, the fresh troops land in Colón, on the Caribbean shore, and need to quickly get to Panama City, on the Pacific Ocean, where the sedition is taking place with US support. The Trans-isthmus railway is an American corporation and is in cahoots with the conspirators, and they refuse to take the Colombian troops to Panama City, agreeing only to take the officers."

"Silly offer, Sombra. It was immediately rejected by the officers, was it not?"

"Well, no, Fierro, as a matter of fact, it was not. The Colombian officers agreed to travel alone, expecting their troops to arrive on the next trainload."

"Sombra, even a traffic policeman would not agree to be deprived of his whistle! Why did these officers agree to be separated from their armed soldiers?"

Fierro, our peoples are class-oriented. The American railway company played the class-card: officers first, soldiers later—and the Colombian officers fell into their own trap."

"Did those Colombian officers really believed they were better than their soldiers?"[3]

"Only God knows, *Fierro*. The fact is that upon arrival in Panama, the Colombian officers were arrested by General Huertas López."

"Wait a minute, Sombra, was he not Colombian, too?"

"Precisely. Huertas had changed sides!"

"Another traitor!"

"That sums it up pretty well, Fierro. But some will see it differently. Huertas López was only twenty-six, and he was ambitious. He already had a Panamanian family, and the seditious Panamanians offered him a high position in the Republic-to-be. General Huertas López certainly had no scruples, and perhaps there were no limits to his treachery. Had he been French and in France he could have perhaps aspired to be a Talleyrand and, like Talleyrand, taken colossal bribes for the settling of new frontiers.[4]

[3] See Namier once more (1963, 153).

[4] Namier (1963, 10).

Which is what he did in Panama; but because he was in Panama, he is remembered, abroad, for having been a crook. In Panama he is a hero."

"He sold out, Sombra, he simply sold out!"

"Money seems to have been mentioned; he certainly had a good life after those events, and even died, at sixty-seven years of age, claiming that he had made Panama."[5]

"So, another coward who was rewarded! Sombra, how can these people trust anyone?"

"That is precisely my point. The poor Colombian harebrained fellow left in charge of the Colombian troops in Colón."

"Who's that, Sombra?"

"The one whose name you do not want to hear again, Fierro!"

"Oh that coward, yes. What about him? By the way, I don't want to hear the name of this other coward again, either!"

"Back to the first coward, Fierro."

"Yes, what about him?"

"How could he make the decision to fire or not to fire on the US troops if he probably guessed right that the only one capable of arresting the recently arrived Colombian officers in Panama was the Colombian General Huertas he reported to?"

> Farmers know what they are fighting for: the land under their feet, the sustenance of their families. Merchants are never so sure.

"He may have guessed correctly, Sombra, but he did not know, right?"

"I am not sure, Fierro."

"Even if he knew that his General had changed sides, who did this first coward owe his allegiance to, his cowardly General or Colombia?"

"Colombia for sure, Fierro, why?"

"Because for Colombia he should had fired on the American invaders."

"You are correct, Fierro. But is that not asking too much from a person who was not tailored to be a hero?"

"It is not, Sombra! It was his duty to shoot."

5 Personal e-mail communication with Ricardo Arias Calderón, August 3, 2009.

"But Sombra, be reasonable; Machiavelli had already warned the Prince about entrusting his defense to waged soldiers. They are unfit for the job because they are arrogant to their own and cowards to the enemy, forever finicky during peace and jittery when war approaches."[6]

"Precisely, Sombra, professionals are not necessarily patriots. One can hardly fathom an army of dentists! If you want a patriot you look for them among those who have something to lose if they lose."

"Like whom, Fierro?"

"Like farmers, Sombra!"[7]

> By seceding from Colombia and selling off the canal rights to America, the new Panamanians neutralized all canal options through other territories, because America would be the greatest beneficiary of any canal in that region. They locked America in through a canal with locks. Quite clever of them, in fact.

"You've got a point there, Fierro. That same land gave us a true hero, Victoriano Lorenzo, a peasant. He fought bravely and was tricked into an ambush."

"Was he killed?"

"Worse, Fierro, he was put before a firing squadron, barely six months before the cowardly incident we were discussing!"

"Good gracious me! Sombra!" said Fierro, crossing himself. "What's wrong with these people?"

"A century later they will still be working it out, Fierro. In the meantime traitors wrote their own history where they portray themselves as patriots."

"But who were they, Sombra?"

"Fierro, they were people who believed they had the right to run government but were not up to competing for higher political echelons within the Colombian Government."

[6] Machiavelli (2008, 131–33).

[7] "For men rooted in the soil, there is, as a rule, a hierarchy of allegiances: to their village community or estate, to their district, to their county—for them the nation is of a naturally federal structure. Traditional beliefs and hereditary ties persist; class and the way of living determine alignments; things are individual and concrete in the village or the small, old-fashioned town" (Namier, 1963, 37).

"So, they identified a new Republic of their own and distributed positions in government to the likes of themselves?"

"You summed it up well, Fierro. One became President, another Minister of Justice, and so on and so forth. They wrote their own history. Even General Huertas is glorified with a passage named after him at Las Bóvedas, in Panama City's Casco Viejo district."

"Sombra, you mean to say that children at school are told that the traitors are the heroes?"

"In short, yes, Fierro. By seceding and selling off the rights to the United States, they neutralized all canal options through other territories, because the United States would be the greatest beneficiary of any canal in that region.[8] They locked in the United States through a canal with locks. Quite clever of them, in fact."

"All crooks are clever, Sombra, but in this case, the Panamanians must have sold themselves cheap."

"Why do you say that, Fierro?"

"Because they had no alternative but to sell themselves out for less than what the Colombians had already rejected!"

> Panama is a land run mostly by merchants. Allegiances are short-lived and run thinner among merchants than they do among farmers. Merchants never know where their next dollar is coming from, so they are inclined to keep in good terms with all who look like their pockets are well lined. It is in the nature of their business.

"Indeed, that is what happened.[9] How would you know, Fierro?"

"Well, it should be obvious, is it not, Sombra? But forget the business side of the deal. Are the children told that it is fair to sell off land that ought to be sacred and which, for the same reason, is not yours?"

[8] *The Economist* (1879).

[9] "The United States used its military leverage to force newly independent Panama into accepting a payment for the use of its territory that was far smaller than the previous agreement which had been freely negotiated between Colombia and the French-owned Panama Canal Company. In fact, it was smaller than the American offer Colombia had previously rejected" (Maurer & Yu, 2006, 2).

"Not precisely in those words, but, yes, Fierro."

"And I hear, Sombra, that all this was pushed through with the gimmick of a power of attorney issued to a French lobbyist who had not set foot in Panama for seventeen years"

"Yes, Fierro."[10]

"But this can only generate a land run by mercenaries, Sombra. A land where allegiances will be bought and sold like any other commodity!"

"As I told you, Fierro, a century later Panamanians will still be working it out. The damage was done; Panama was born out of an original sin. Honorable people will spring up here and there, and someday they will be the majority and rewrite their history and demolish the monuments that now salute the filibusters, and a new paradigm will be born in Panama."

"Who would do it, Sombra?"

"Most likely a woman will, Fierro.

"Why a woman. Sombra?"

"Because one of their women is worth ten of their men."

"Anyone in particular, Sombra?"

"Ana Elena Porras might just make it."

"What will it take, Sombra?"

"Building trust, Fierro. There is so little of it to build upon that Panamanians cannot even coalesce around team sports."

"Not even for play Fierro?"

"At least not enough to build stadiums for the games, until well into the twentieth century, Fierro."

"I cannot wait to set this right, Sombra!"

"Fierro, people like you have tried and have been misunderstood. It will take a grassroots movement. But you touched the crux of the matter; this land is one run mostly by merchants. Allegiances are short-lived and run thinner among merchants than they do among farmers."

"Scoundrels!"

[10] Indeed, Philippe Buneau Varilla was the representative of the New Interocean Canal Company, which owned the rights granted to the initial foiled French operation led by Ferdinand de Lesseps. After Panama's secession, M. Buneau Varilla was appointed Panama's ambassador to America and he signed the concession for the Canal with American Secretary Hay.

"Some are, indeed, Fierro, and they will provide safe-haven for thieves, drug-traffickers, corrupt public officials and many more."

"How will they get away with it?"

"Through their lawyers, Fierro."[11]

"A facón would clear their minds, Sombra, reminding them of the honorability associated with family names!"

"Only if society paid attention to such niceties, Fierro. Merchants never know where the next dollar is coming from, so they are inclined to stay on good terms with all who look like their pockets are well lined. It is in the nature of their business. Remember how the Portuguese became merchants?"

"That makes it a dangerous land, Sombra! Let us move on."

> Maquiavel had already warned the Prince about entrusting his defense to waged soldiers. They are unfit for the job because they are arrogant to their own and cowards to the enemy, forever finicky during peace and jittery when war approaches. That is why, during a hostile take-over, you should not rely on the support of the mercenaries you have lined their pockets with fat bonuses during more peaceful times.

"Only dangerous if you let your principles interfere with your goals, Fierro."

"Well, it is enough for me, Sombra, my Spinoza cannot take any more treachery. He wants us to gallop ahead!" As Spinoza galloped, he neighed: "*Non tantum mortis damnetur, ejusque bona proscribantur, sed ut supplicii aliquod signum in aeternam rei memoriam in publico emineat.*"[12]

"You may be right, Fierro! We are closer to hell than heaven, and we should not slow down when passing so close to hell!"[13]

[11] The 2016 scandal known as Panama Papers provides ample evidence of services offered by one of Panama's largest providers: Mossak and Fonseca (Harding, 2016).

[12] "Not only is he [the treacherous one] to be condemned to death, and his goods confiscated, but some sign of his punishment must remain visible in public for an eternal memorial of the event" (Spinoza, 1667, Caput VIII, paragraph XXV). For an English translation, see https://ebooks.adelaide.edu.au/s/spinoza/benedict/political/. Both accessed January 2, 2017.

[13] Soto, Benjamin. "Riding through hell." Lyrics at http://www.metrolyrics.com/riding-through-hell-lyrics-heavenly.html. Accessed January 3, 2017.

## Costa Rica

By sunset Fierro and Sombra had fled past Panama and had arrived in Costa Rica, where they decided to give their horses a rest.

Costa Rica, since its early Spanish days, has been a land of peaceful farmers. Mechanic activities, in the sense that they are repetitive, are unlikely to breed the background for heroism to rise. Heroes, in such societies, are likely to be depicted against the background of unusual activities. That was the case of Juan Santamaría.[14]

An American filibuster, by the name of Walter Walkins, had carved for himself a territory out of Nicaragua, where he exercised complete control. Expansionist by nature, Walkins invaded neighboring Costa Rica in 1856, where his forces outnumbered the local militia. He would have taken over were it not for Juan Santamaría's resolve in torching Walkins's refuge and forcing him to retreat. Santamaría himself succumbed to the ordeal, after asking his fellow countrymen not to forget his mother. This is, of course, an unfair summary of a heroic event, but it suffices for our purposes.

"What do we have at hand? asked Fierro, impatiently."

"A humble Mr. Juan Santamaría, Fierro."

"What about him, Sombra?"

"He would not have been remembered for long, Fierro, except for one single and most challenging task he took upon himself to perform."

"What about him, Sombra?"

"Fierro, Santamaría offered no less than his life for his country."

> "History is written by the victors. There may be heroes on both sides, but only the victors are paid homage to. If Walkins had won, despite Santamaría's martyrdom, we are unlikely to have heard of Santamaría."

"Some progress compared to the earlier scoundrels, Sombra; but you see, Santamaría was a farmer, for the occasion dressed as a drummer."

"Indeed, Fierro, a farmer, of course. In risking his life for his country he performed the act of a

[14] This section on Juan Santamaría loosely follows the arguments brought forward by Danuta Mozejko (1988).

hero, and following generations paid tribute to his life because, in essence, Santamaría's altruism turned all Costa Ricans into his debtors."

"What became of his legacy, Sombra?"

"Fierro, Santamaría, from a humble peasant, turned into a greater man, perfect for all purposes, and the image of what all men ought to be like in similar circumstances."

"Precisely the opposite of the other neighboring scoundrels whose names I have already forgotten, Sombra!"

"You are right, Fierro, and note that Santamaría's deed surely benefits the collective. Cultures cannot produce heroes out of individuals seeking their own private benefit; there must be an abnegation involved, preferably involving martyrdom, so fitting of our collective religious heritage. This is the difference between Santamaría and the traitors in Panama and Colombia whose names of which you wish not to be reminded."

"How is Santamaría the peasant transformed into this most unlikely image of a hero, Sombra?"

"Society does that, Fierro, through its instruments—its historians, its press, authorities who commend statues, uncovered at Alajuela in 1891—and pay homage to Santamaría's deed."

"Still today, Sombra?"

"Still today. Nobel laureate and President of Costa Rica, gave a speech next to Santamaría's statue at Alajuela in 1987."

"Why do they do it, Sombra?"

"So that he will be emulated, Fierro! Santamaría, the humble peasant who until then led an uneventful life, was raised to the

### The Cost of Panama's Original Sin

It will take Panama more than a century to have a proper mail system, to have a symphonic orchestra, or even a ballet troupe; because they never quite owned their place. They didn't even own Panama when they sold it. Siphoning the profits out was the most they could do, and through their example they taught the rest to do the same.

You cannot run a business on a lie. Lying may enable you to reap a quick buck here and there, but not much more than that because people do not like being cheated. They cheat you back, when you are lucky. Everybody does, from your customers to your employees. The original sin is a hard burden to carry.

position of a hero by his own people. His heroism is remembered in perpetuity, for it is in society's interest to be able to request all its sons and daughters to emulate Santamaría's behavior when need be."

"Indeed, to Juan Santamaría all Costa Ricans are perpetually indebted, Sombra!"

"Yes, this is why Santamaría's own deathbed request of 'do not forget my mother' was remembered as a debt and dutifully paid by granting a pension to his mother!"

"Good for Costa Rica! I could settle and have a farm here, Sombra!"

"That's the purpose of honoring the debt to Santamaría, Fierro."

"Why, Sombra?"

"By paying the debt to Santamaría, Fierro, Costa Rica recognizes that the debt existed and needs to be honored. Even the recognition of this debt to his surviving mother underwrites the request for emulation desired in the deification of the hero. This is what makes a land an honorable one, one where people will want to live."

"True, Sombra, it feels good to be here."

"Precisely, for in the hero's request—not to forget his mother—there is a gesture of tenderness that approximates the hero to the familiar and the family world, helping everybody to appreciate the hero as 'one of us,' and therefore binding all into the collective debt that must be repaid, by emulation if not by money."

"I cannot help feeling sorry for Gumercindo, Sombra. Why doesn't Brazil pay homage to him like Costa Rica does to Santamaría?"

"Because Gumercindo lost, Fierro."

"So what? He was a hero nonetheless."

"True, but history is written by the victors. There may be heroes on both sides, but only the victors are paid homage. If Walkins had won, despite Santamaría's martyrdom, we are unlikely to have heard of Santamaría."

"Very unfair, Sombra. It is no way to build an honorable society, because one can win dishonorably, too, you know? I have won duels after throwing dirt in my enemy's eyes, blinding him before the final blow.[15] I'm not proud of that, Sombra, but it is me speaking to you, not my enemy."

"I know, Fierro. We all know that dishonor frequently pays and it shows in the ways that some people have become exceedingly rich."

## Lesson: Inauthentic Leadership Stunts Organizational Development

"All right, Sombra, we know what happened in both Panama and Costa Rica. What did we learn from this?"

"Fierro, if we look at it from the short-term perspective, the lesson to be drawn is one thing. In the longer term, it is another."

"Sombra! Don't mystify!"

"The canal paid to the ones who built it, but they had to carry on their shoulders a society that could not mature because it was still-born. The same happens at the *saladeros*, Fierro. If you cannot trust your leaders you do not engage in their battles, and all loose."

"Fierro, people living in Panama had attempted secession several times. This time they won."

If you have not earned your land fighting for it, you would be unsure of your right to it. The scoundrels that sold off Panama intimately knew their position was weak. They may have built statues for themselves, named streets after them, but they knew what they had done and that their flimsy power rested in somebody else's hands. These people intimately knew that their power could be challenged and that they might lose it all. This is why they lived on a land but built elsewhere.

[15] See stanzas 276 and 277 of *Martin Fierro*, http://www.gutenberg.org/files/14765/14765–8.txt. Accessed January 3, 2017. Translated in the *Gaucho Martin Fierro*, adapted from the Spanish and rendered into English verse by Walter Owen (1936, 69).

"But not by fighting, Sombra! That is the difference. It was a business outcome in which not all took part!"

"True, it is an important difference, and perhaps the only difference one should look at."

"So, shall we move on to Costa Rica?"

"Not yet, Fierro, let me extend myself a little more on this case."

"A little, then, Sombra."

"You see, Fierro, there were many canals about to be built, not all through what is now known as the Republic of Panama. But only one would be built because once a canal was built that would prevent another one being built for at least a century."

"So?"

"Fierro, had a canal been built through Nicaragua, the people in Panama would have lost the benefit of diverting to their area a significant part of world sea traffic."

"It was Colombia who would have lost, Sombra!"

"True, Fierro, but benefits of a canal expand like ripples in a pond; they are larger at the center. People in Panama would have benefited most from the canal. Colombians had other things going for them, they would not depend on a canal as much as the Panamanians would."

"Yes, Sombra, I can see that people in Panama would have more to lose in a negotiation with the United States that was being handled by Colombia."

"Precisely, Fierro. People in Panama must have thought that the Colombians were asking too high a price for a canal from the Americans, because the Colombians could afford to wait longer."

"So they offered to allow a canal for less?"

"I think they did, Fierro. They ended up paying a high price for it, in that the country was then split by a canal."

"But in not being farmers, they probably cared less, Sombra!"

"I think you are right, Sombra. The ones who did not earn much from all of this were the farmers in the hinterland. They had to put up with a government they were given no voice in, and which concentrated the revenue into a social class in a way that it perpetuated itself in power for a century."

"Was there anything positive about this ordeal, Sombra?"

"There are better overall sanitary conditions in Panama than elsewhere in the region, a spin-off of the building of the canal and the fighting of malaria and yellow fever, but otherwise, not much."

"Sombra, but did not the revenue of traffic along the canal turn that strip of land into El Dorado?"

"Except for a neighborhood in Panama City with that name, no, it did not."

"Why not, Sombra?"

"Well, that is the price of the original sin, Fierro."

"In what sense?"

"It will take Panama more than a century to have a proper mail system, a symphonic orchestra, or even a ballet troupe, Fierro."

"I see, they never quite owned the place."

"No, they did not even own it when they sold it, so they knew they too could end up at the wrong end of a gun, anytime. The most they could do was to siphon the profits out; and through their example, they taught the rest to do the same. Fierro, the original sin is a heavy weight to carry."

"An awful one too, Sombra. So, are you suggesting that the behavior has a meaning for the conduct of business?"

"Indeed I am. You cannot run a business on a lie, Fierro. It may enable you to reap a quick buck here and there, but not much more than that because people do not like being cheated. They cheat you back, when you are lucky."

"Who cheats back, Sombra?"

"Everybody does, from your customers to your employees, Fierro."[16]

"And in Costa Rica, what happened?"

"Well, you can figure out that one for yourself, can't you, Sombra?"

"Yes, I guess they are a people who can be proud of their past."

[16] McGovern and Moon (2007).

"And sure of their roots and of the entitlement to the land where they stand, Fierro. Costa Ricans built a country. Panamanians built a shopping center. This is why in the long run, selling off did not pay, except to the few who pocketed the initial proceeds and positioned themselves to reap the flow of future income."

"Did it pay to the ones who bought them off, Sombra?"

"It did, but they had to carry on their shoulders a society that could not mature because it was stillborn. The same happens at the saladeros, Fierro. If you cannot trust your leaders, you do not engage in their battles, and all lose."

# 10

## Fierro and Sombra Discuss the Leadership of the Mexican Revolution

"What's this, Sombra?"

"You are close to your father's land, Fierro. This is Mexico."

"Who are those people?"

"They follow Emiliano Zapata. Had you been born close to your father's land you are likely to have been fighting on their side, Fierro!"

"Not on Pancho Villa's side, Sombra?"

"No, Villa supporters are in the North of Mexico."

"You name your horse after the horse of Felipe Ángeles, who joined Pancho Villa. Would we have been enemies, Sombra?"

"Only uneasy allies, Fierro."

"What goes on here?"

"It's been going on for a long time. Perhaps even before the Spanish arrived, Fierro."

"But why do we now have people that look like brothers fighting each other, Sombra?"

"The story is as old as mankind. They fight for power, Fierro, and neither Villa nor Zapata will win, despite being the peoples' most loved autochthonous leaders. Nor will their most prepared acolyte, Felipe Ángeles, win,."

"Who is that one leading a cannon bombardment, Fierro?"

"That's my man, Ángeles."

"Yours for any particular reason, Sombra?"

"Perhaps because I believe he was honest, educated, loyal and sought the best for all; not much more than that."

"Was he good with the facón, Sombra?"

"I don't think so. He was too good with cannons to bother with the facón, Fierro."

"All men are brave when standing alongside a cannon, Sombra! What I am asking is, did this Ángeles know when to hold his ground?"

"I think he did, Fierro. He was a studied professional military man. He studied artillery at a French military academy, thus his penchant for naming his horses with the names of French generals."

"You are telling me nothing I want to know, Sombra! What evidence do you have that this man held his ground?"

"He risked his life in supporting President Madero."

"Well, we are getting closer now, Sombra. Why did he choose to side with Madero instead of with Madero's enemies?"

"Because Ángeles was a loyal military man, Fierro. President Madero was the constitutional president, and Ángeles could not see himself siding with those who wanted to illegally topple Madero."

"Did Ángeles stand to lose everything—his life, his family, his possessions—and still back Madero?"

"Yes, Fierro, that's Ángeles in a nutshell. Huerta toppled Madero and had him killed. Huerta would have killed Ángeles, too, had he not believed that would have brought him too much trouble with the North Americans."

"I can see why you like him, Sombra. But why would the North Americans side with Ángeles?"

"They must have seen a future ally in him, Fierro. Someone they could trust."

"Because he was likely to betray Mexicans, Sombra?"

"He did not betray Madero, Fierro, why would he side with foreigners?"

"So many do, Sombra; Americans are wealthier, we just saw how Panama was brought into being."

"True, but it is mostly merchants who change sides at the flip of a coin, not the military, certainly not the Mexican military brought up at the Colegio Militar, which Ángeles directed. No,

Fierro, Ángeles was an honest man caught in the vice of history. Madero had replaced Porfirio Diaz; whose will was Mexican law for almost four decades."

"That's a long time, Sombra. Diaz must have been good with the facón!"

"If not with the facón, he was good at balancing his act, a bit like Venezuela's Juan Vicente Gómez. Porfirio Díaz was a good organizer and had a strong hand, but at the end he weakened."

"Weakening is the first sign of an impending demise, Sombra!"

"You are right, Fierro. Madero took over but Huerta snatched power away from him, with US support if you wish."

"Why so easily, Sombra?"

"It wasn't easy, Fierro, but it did not take long, either. US President Taft was tricked into intervening in Mexico by his ambassador to Mexico, Henry Lane, who was linked to big American business. William Randolph Hearst, of the American newspaper industry, was fearful that an insurrection in Mexican Chihuahua might threaten his cattle interests there."

"Sombra, Hearst had invested at a risk, had he not?"

"True, Fierro, but people do not like to lose money, and those with the most money are the most dangerous ones. President Madero regretfully relied on Huerta to quell the rebellion."

"Did Madero suspect that Huerta would do him in, Sombra?"

"President Madero was a trusting man, perhaps he did not suspect the outcome, but it is telling that he sought Ángeles's support at the time."

"Why, then, did Madero not want to rely on Huerta, Sombra?"

"It may sound foolish, but President Madero did not like Huerta."

"Do you need to like your henchman, Sombra?"

"No, but Madero had principles and was rather inflexible about it."

"Huerta lacked principles, Sombra?"

"To President Madero he did, yes. President Madero was a teetotaler and Huerta was a drunkard; but that was not all."

"What else, Sombra?"

"President Madero was a refined man of European ancestry."

"And of course, Huerta was not, Sombra. Was he of native extraction?"

"Precisely."

"So, was it not the old racial discrimination thing at play, Sombra?"

"Hard to tell now, Fierro. But it may have had some bearing."

"So, what's new Sombra? The Indian brute pulled the rebellion off and American big business paid him off with his own Mexico! To hell with Madero and the honest election that brought him to office! Taft himself was behind this![1] Mince no words, Sombra! That is what happened!"

"Well, that is what it boiled down to, yes, Fierro!"

"What happened next, Sombra?"

"Huerta fulfilled the drunkard brute prophecy after all, taking all power for himself, and that unleashed uprisings in the North with Pancho Villa and Venustiano Carranza, and in the South with Emiliano Zapata."

"Tell me more about these, Sombra."

"These, Fierro, are about the most interesting fellows to turn up in recent Mexican history."

"More, and be quick, Sombra!"

"They were all of native extraction. Zapata commanded the South and Center of Mexico, Pancho Villa the North and Center, and Don Venustiano Carranza in the Northeast was a man at the fringes of the political system."

"You mean to say 'with a chip on his shoulder'?"

"In a way, yes. Don Venustiano was older, a governor of Coahuila, and ripe for larger challenges, like the Presidency. No other character passed into Mexican history with the title of *Don*; at the time he did not dislike being called *Primer Jefe*, either."

"What separated them, Sombra?"

"As I said earlier, Fierro. Regionalism split Emiliano Zapata from Pancho Villa. Mexico is a long country, along a North-South axis. Small landholdings predominate in the tropical South, where the natives faced the encroachment of the farmers of European ancestry. Large cattle ranches predominate in the more arid North, with closer links to the United States. Different problems impinged upon the priority of the solutions to be sought."

"Nice try, Sombra. But what were the solutions sought?"

[1] Aguilar and Meyer (1993, 33–34).

"Zapata's own solutions tasted of extreme agrarianism to those of the North. Zapata appealed to the left-wingers with Pancho, but not to the larger landowners also with him, like Maytorena of Sonora, who yearned to return to the exploitation of the ranches confiscated from the Porfiristas."

"Was that all, Sombra?"

"Not all, of course. There are the personal issues to deal with. Pancho was not an institution-building man. The most he could envisage was an agrarian warrior colony. Comrades would work there three days a week, teach others how to fight, and, like US minutemen, always be ready to defend their land and sustenance at the shortest call.[2] Among Pancho's group were the most unruly ones. Pancho did not seek any public position because he would not know what to do with it; he actually told Zapata so at Xochimilco."[3]

"And Zapata? Sombra, did Zapata not jump at the opportunity?"

"No, he did not, he agreed with Pancho. He was comfortable enough with letting their allies take care of government as long as they created no more problems for them when the machetes would fall on their heads."

"That's my man, Sombra! You see? I told you so! Zapata knows how to clear a man's mind! Machete, facón, same thing!"

"I thought you would like him, Fierro. He was a bit of a brute, like you!"

"And Don Venustiano, Sombra?"

"Fierro, what needs to be said is that this man was older, more reserved, and conservative, as befits an old landlord and Porfirista senator."

"That's all, Sombra?"

"Yes, Fierro, those are three of the four protagonists shaping Mexico: Villa, Zapata and Carranza."

"Who's the fourth, Sombra, your Felipe Ángeles?"

"I wish he were, Fierro, but no, the fourth protagonist is the backdrop: the United States."

"What do you mean, Sombra?"

[2] In a conversation with Paul Reed, picked up by Aguilar and Meyer (1993, 42–43).

[3] Aguilar and Meyer (1993, 56).

"The threat of US intervention lingered on during all this period, Fierro."

"That should have been enough to alert the three protagonists to how much they had to lose, Sombra. Look at what happened to the Colombians by losing Panama to the United States."

"Precisely, Fierro. The US backdrop acts like a container of Mexican behavior."

"Mexicans had already lost to the United States all what is now the Southwestern United States, had they not, Sombra?"

"Only sixty years before, Fierro."

"Could it happen again, Sombra?"

"Unlikely. The United States was more concerned with its interests in Europe at the time, when its allies were not doing well in a war against Germany."

"Tell me more, Sombra."

"Fierro, the United States was being called in to support Britain, but it was reluctant to intervene in a war it did not see as its own."

"But if it did enter the war, would it have made a difference?"

"The Germans certainly thought it would, Fierro, so they moved to preempt the United States' entry into the war they had a handsome chance of winning if the United States did not join on Britain's side."

"How, Sombra?"

"By enticing the Mexicans to invade the United States to recoup about half the territories lost earlier to the Americans, Fierro!"

"Amazing, Sombra! How would that have been achieved?"

"Fierro, it was a chess move. In order to divert US attention to its Southern frontier, and away from the war in Europe, the German Empire, on January 16, 1917, through its Foreign Secretary Arthur Zimmerman, offered weapons and financial support to the Mexicans, supporting its annexation of Southern United States."

"Sombra, the Germans were paying with what the Mexicans thought was theirs in any case."

"True, Fierro, the Mexicans wanted it badly, and it would have helped Carranza to unite Mexicans into a war of self-respect. This is what the Germans were counting on."

"What happened, Sombra?"

"Not much, Fierro. The telegram was deciphered by the British, who used it to lure the Americans into the European war on the Allied side, which happened barely ten weeks after the telegram was received by the Mexicans."[4]

"Wonderful piece of fouled strategy, Sombra! It was so fast it did not allow the Mexicans to do much. Did they?"

"Not much, Fierro. Carranza apparently instructed one of his generals to gauge the feasibility of the move, but his general was not impressed."

"Why not, Sombra?"

"Because the German financial assistance would mostly be needed to purchase weapons to fight the Americans, but the Americans were the only arms suppliers on this side of the world."

"Of course, Sombra! But the Germans also offered weapons."

"Yes, they did, Fierro, but the British controlled much of maritime transportation, and it would have been too risky for the Mexicans to enter into war with the United States relying on an unsteady supply of German weaponry."

"So, the telegram backfired, Sombra. It enticed the Mexicans only a little, and it accelerated the US entry into the war on the British side."

"Precisely, Fierro. But you see, the focus of US interests would always be crucial to the Mexicans, who, in being too close to the United States, 'felt too far from God.' "[5]

"But, Sombra, was it not Porfirio Díaz who said something like that?"

"Indeed, Fierro, the same Porfirio who Madero succeeded. Those who chased off Madero's killer would still be haunted by the same imperialist backdrop. It will not go away Fierro!"

"Indeed, and it was in the United States' mind when recommending President Taft to put an end to Madero's rule; remember, Sombra?"

"How could I forget? Nasty, Fierro, nasty."

[4] National Archives of the United States http://www.archives.gov/education/lessons/zimmermann/. Accessed January 3, 2017.

[5] The often-quoted phrase is "Poor Mexico, so far from God, so close to the United States" (Goodman, 2009).

"But my Spinoza is getting jittery already; I had better go."

"There is nowhere to go, Fierro."

"There is, I came to see my father; remember, Sombra?"

"Go ahead. Leave Spinoza with me and ride a donkey, Fierro. A bucking Spinoza would probably dismount you in Comala, the mouth of hell."

"What will you do, Sombra?"

"I will wait for you at the Battle of Zacatecas, where Felipe Ángeles defeated Huerta's men."

"Will I return, Sombra?"

"You will, Fierro, all men must move forward. Follow that man on a donkey, he will give you directions."

They parted. Fierro returned a few days later and met Sombra at Zacatecas. The kind reader may turn to Juan Rulfo's *Pedro Páramo* for Fierro's lone adventure in the body of his half-brother, Luciano Preciado.

"When people are cheated repeatedly they become skeptic survivors, Fierro. They narrow their interests to those immediately relevant to their families. Fernando de Fuentes's film, *El Compadre Mendoza*, was not worse than most. Mendoza managed to keep his hacienda by lavishly attending Huerta's troops after also lavishly attending Zapata's own."

"Found your father, Fierro?"

"Sombra, I have been to a hellish desert on a donkey with no name![6] That man, the one who you pointed out as capable of giving me directions—he was dead!"

"So are we, Fierro!"

"Sombra! It was hot and he spoke with a whisper; three crows flew over us and their crowing almost prevented me from hearing what he said."

"But did he point the way to Comala, Fierro?"

"He led me to Comala all right; where they were all dead! But alive too, Sombra!"

"Nothing new, Fierro, what about your father?"

"I didn't like him, Sombra."

[6] May be read to the tune of Dewey Bunnell's 1972 song "A horse with no name." Lyrics at http://www.accessbackstage.com/america/song/song005.htm. Accessed January 3, 2017.

"Why, Fierro?"

"He was mean to my half-brother's mother. He loved only one woman, Susana San Juan. Even then he mostly wanted total possession of her body."

"Most men do, Fierro, few even realize when they are in love."

"He was mean to men, too, Sombra. He used people."

"He must have been powerful, Fierro."

"He was powerful because the rest were weak, Sombra. They all sold out! Even Father Rentería did."

"Nobody stood up against him, Fierro?"

"A few did, Sombra, and he had them all killed, through his henchman El Tilcuate."

"When people are cheated repeatedly, they become skeptic survivors, Fierro. They narrow their interests to those immediately relevant to their families. Mendoza managed to keep his hacienda by lavishly attending Huerta's troops after also lavishly attending Zapata's own."[7]

"I don't know about Mendoza, Sombra. What we don't know doesn't hurt us as much. But my father was too devious! Pedro Páramo bribed and infiltrated the revolutionary forces intent on changing matters."

"They cannot have been that intent if they were bribed, Fierro. It sounds like Pedro Páramo was no worse than El Compadre. Not an excuse, but not worse, either."

"Few had much idea of what they were doing, Sombra. Even another henchman, Sucuri, chose to join the rebel group led by Father Rentería and not the other group only because he liked the way they shouted more!"

"They must have sounded like a montonera! It is your chance to live your life again, Fierro, for every end is only a new beginning."

"You are right that they sounded like a montonera, the same fierce joy. I almost joined them, too. So compelling, Sombra!"

"You are too old for that, Fierro."

"What do you mean by old? I am dead, Sombra. I ought to be timeless."

"Precisely, there is no point in joining them now, Fierro, except as bystanders, the living must learn on their own. Let us now watch

[7] Fuentes (1934).

Ángeles at Zacatecas. And, by the way, the only father image you should care about is the one you carry with you; learn and pass it on."

"What is going on here, Sombra? The sound of the cannons is deafening!"

"Are you uncomfortable, Fierro? Imagine what it must be like for those fellows handling the cannons!"

"It must be even worse to those at the other end, Sombra!"

"True, Fierro, and Ángeles has deployed his cannons just behind the cover of a mountain. The other side cannot see and shoot at his cannons. They must only withstand the barrage!"

"Clever move by Ángeles, Sombra!"

"This is why I wanted you to see this, Fierro. Ángeles is the only one on the insurrection side to have studied and made a profession out of killing through cannons."

"I can see the effectiveness of it, Sombra, but I cannot see much courage in it."

Suddenly, there was an explosion barely ten feet away.

"Look, Fierro! Ángeles and Villa, their horses and aides—all have been toppled to the ground!"

"I can't see much, Sombra! There is a black cloud covering all!"

"Yes, Fierro, and there is a hideous stench of gunpowder, too!"

"What happened, Sombra?"

"A grenade exploded here, the *metraille* run through us but look there, Fierro! Look at the soldiers handling the cannon!"

"I am beginning to see them, Sombra, the black cloud is now dissipating! But wait, Sombra, they are all dead! Look at their expressions of horror!"

"Yes, Fierro, one is headless, another lost his two hands and the bones of his forearms are exposed!"

"What happened here, Sombra?"

"Their own grenade exploded in their arms as it was being handled, Fierro!"

"Horrible, Sombra!"

"So you still think these poor devils need no courage, Fierro!"

"Horrible, Sombra!"

"Look, Fierro, Ángeles and Villa are picking themselves up! They are alive!"

"Sombra, Ángeles is haranguing the survivors! He is shouting at them!"

"Yes, Fierro, he is telling them not to waste time mourning their dead or they will all be killed!"

"Villa is crying, Sombra! He is weeping for his soldiers, killed by their own grenades; he says it is too hard to bear!"

"This is warfare with artillery, Fierro; massively deadly, arbitrary, indiscriminate. Tell me now, Fierro, tell me now that you need not courage to face cannon fire!"

"More than courage, Sombra, you need faith to advance under cannon fire while your soul trembles and your knees refuse to hold your weight."

"This is what Ángeles would say, Fierro, he pitied his men, wrought to be peasants, not heroes, but who would still behave like heroes."

"What is all the fuss about now, Sombra?"

"Villa's troops have made advances, Fierro, and the cannons need to be repositioned."

"But, Sombra, look at Villa, Ángeles, and their top men: They are moving fast as well, under a shower of high-pitched bullets that sound like mosquitoes!"

"That they must do if they want to keep control of what goes on in the battlefield. Fierro, this is not face-to-face facón fighting. Instead of physical strength and reflexes, there is a lot of brain that goes into this business."

"I concede that, Sombra. But what I have most difficulty with is the sheer arbitrariness of who gets killed or maimed or comes back unscathed. That is hard to fathom, and I think it is also unfair and indecent."

"You may be right, Fierro. Pay attention now. Villa's side has won,

Felipe Ángeles' cannonade at Zacatecas signaled the beginning of the end of Huerta.

Fierro argued that triumph through the cannon also signals the end of honor, because as in a bullfight, it is not in the killing that honor is expressed, but in man's disposition to put his life at stake at it. On the other hand, there is nothing honorable about gambling one's life at the wrong end of the cannon. A cannon's metraille kills randomly and battles last for days while corpses rot in the fields. In a cannon war people may even die of disease rather than fighting!

Fierro argued that face-to-face fighting sorts the good from the bad more efficiently too. Matters are over in a couple of hours at the most, luck plays a lesser role than in battles fought with cannons.

his enemy is firing less frequently, and soon we will see all Villa's army rejoicing."

"What about, Sombra?"

"Life, Fierro! For being alive, for having been spared! They will celebrate that first, then for having won! And Ángeles will tour the battlefield to inspect and learn. Let us move closer and stay at his side."

"Sombra, Villa's army is already rejoicing. But they have probably soiled their pants."

"Who cares, Fierro! They are alive, and this is the beginning of the end of Huerta!"

"Also the end of honor, Sombra!"

"Nonsense, honor is not only expressed when killing a man with a facón, Fierro!"

"You still don't get it, Sombra! Like in a bullfight, it is not in the killing that honor is expressed, but in a man's disposition to put his life at stake at it![8] There is nothing honorable about gambling one's life at the wrong end of the cannon, whichever end that may be!"

"Fine, Fierro, but move on. Ángeles is shooting a wounded horse and complains that he can hardly hear the noise of his revolver, so deaf he has become from the explosions echoed in the mountains, which have magnified the tempest of lead and steel."

"They complain about the stench of the dead, too, Sombra. It's nauseating. They have been fighting for a couple of days over this land and there are unburied corpses lying all over the place."

"What did you expect, Fierro?"

"Face-to-face fighting sorts the good from the bad more efficiently. Matters are over in a couple of hours at the most; luck plays a lesser role than here. Sombra, in this war people may even die of disease rather than from fighting!"

"Good point, Fierro! Look at the expression of horror and pain in the faces you can see."

"I hate the randomness of it all, Sombra! God does not play dice!"

[8] As in stanza 263, when Fierro defies the squadron sent to arrest him: "Yo quise hacerles saber/ que allí se hallaba un varón/. Freely translated as "I wanted them to know/ that here a man stood" (Hernández, 2005, 263).

"And yet he might well play, Fierro! Ángeles is musing with Villa now, about the beauty of it all!"

"Beauty, Sombra?"

"Ángeles feels like an orchestra director after a symphonic performance, Fierro. There has been thunder, echoed by the mountains, explosions, fire, high-pitched bullets passing by, yells of despair and of rejoicing, troops advancing and falling, others receding. Fierro, you cannot argue that this is not unique art, though you may not like it!"

"Maimed people all over the place, and that is art, Sombra?"

"But it was all for a purpose, Fierro. Some must die in order that others may live with dignity."

"Forget about it, Sombra. But while you mention it, what was all this massacre for?"

Ángeles left his horse Turena with Pancho Villa and took exile in America, first near the frontier, then further away; always scheming for a way to unite the opposition to Carranza.

In a move that is still bewildering, because it was against most sensible advice Ángeles received, he gave up growing old in America and returned to Mexico to join Villa, mounted on a horse that was no longer named after a French military man but after an American abolitionist hero: John Brown.

"Fierro, this was probably the sole most important battle of the Mexican Revolution. All are important, but many are indecisive. This one consolidated Ángeles as a most competent strategist and convinced Carranza that he had to eliminate Ángeles if he was to become President of Mexico."

"But wasn't Villa backing Ángeles, Sombra?"

"He was, Fierro; but after Zacatecas, Villa—against Ángeles's advice—made many strategic mistakes that wore him down. Not even Ángeles could bring the necessary union between Zapata and Villa to contain Carranza, who ultimately became the *Primer Jefe*."

"What happened to Ángeles, Sombra?"

"He left his horse, Turena, with Pancho Villa and took exile in the United States, first near the frontier, then further away, always scheming for a way to unite the opposition to Carranza."

"Did he succeed, Sombra?"

John Brown's musing over his execution sentence: "at this time, to seal my testimony for God and humanity with my blood will do vastly more toward advancing the cause I have earnestly endeavored to promote, than all I have done in my life before."
Felipe Ángeles own, under similar circumstances: "My death will do the democratic cause better than all my efforts during my life. The blood of the martyrs will fertilize good causes."

"No, Fierro, he did not. But worse, in a move that is still bewildering, because it was against the most sensible advice Ángeles received, he gave up growing old and safe in the United States and came back to Mexico to join Villa, this time mounted on a horse that was no longer named after a French military man but after an American hero: John Brown."[9]

"What happened then, Sombra?"

"Ángeles was betrayed, and executed at Chihuahua after a mock trial, which was ordered by Carranza."

"Why did he return, Sombra?"

"Fierro, remember the Abdón Porte story, the center forward of the Nacional soccer team in Uruguay?"

"Yes, Sombra, the Uruguayan who took his own life in the field in 1918."

"Yes indeed, the Uruguayan. He shot himself at the center of his team's football field when he sensed that during the next season he might be too old to play and might be relegated to the reserves' bench."

From being a lover of things, French Felipe Ángeles turned to love what America stood for. He loved America's freedom and the institutions Americans had put in place to defend them.

"Sombra, you think that Ángeles knew his chances were slim upon his return and that in fact his return was a suicidal act?"[10]

"I do, Fierro. I do. A man of honor, you would say."

"Despite Ángeles being an artilleryman, Sombra?"

[9] In 1859, the abolitionist John Brown led his men to take the US Armory and Arsenal at Harper's Ferry, http://www.civilwar.org/education/history/biographies/john-brown.html. Accessed January 3, 2017.

[10] Katz (1998, 709).

"Oh forget that nonsense, Fierro! Ángeles fought with a longer facón than yours, that's all! Only that when he felt his strength was withering, and that he could no longer aspire to serve the country he had prepared himself to defend, he quit in an honorable way."

"Riding on a horse named after an American, Sombra?"

"Yes, Fierro, which is telling of Ángeles's intellectual evolution."

"Love to the point of allowing annexation, Sombra?"

"Never, Fierro! Ángeles died loving Mexico and Mexicans, and he feared the United States as a neighbor."

"What did he get himself killed for, Sombra?"

"Fierro, Ángeles turned his mock trial into a symbol of his martyrdom for Mexico: 'My death will do the democratic cause more good than all my efforts during my life. The blood of the martyrs will fertilize good causes.'"[11]

"Those sound like John Brown's own words when musing over his execution sentence:

> At this time, to seal my testimony for God and humanity with my blood will do vastly more toward advancing the cause I have earnestly endeavored to promote, than all I have done in my life before.[12]

"Of course, Fierro! Felipe Ángeles vividly expressed his love for his heroes in many ways; naming his horses like them was the most obvious expression of his admiration."

The contenders, with deep roots in their cultures, which made them so effective leaders of their neighbors, did not translate beyond the natural frontiers of their regionalism. Neither Villa nor Zapata could have been effective leaders of a unified Mexico. This is why they did not make it. Felipe Ángeles did not make it either, because he may not have been born to be a leader, but to be a manager. Perhaps Ángeles would have been a leader of a coalition in a more educated México. But at the time of the Mexican Revolution Ángeles's knowledge was perceived as haughtiness. His foreign affiliations may have alienated him further. He had studied in France and had married a Californian lady with whom he had four children. Cold and power-hungry Carranza was clever enough to see in Ángeles an obstacle to his dictatorial inclinations, and had Ángeles killed after a mock trial.

[11] Translation of Felipe Angeles notes when already a prisoner on his way to Chihuahua, where he was executed (Gilly, 2008, 67).

[12] Burghardt Du Bois (1909, 182).

## Lessons on Mexico: Locally Grown Leaders Have the Flavor of Authenticity

"Summing up, Sombra, what do we have here?"

"Fierro, I think we have two issues to draw on, both bearing on foreign leadership and alignment. We had three autochthonous leaders with strong followings: Villa, Zapata and Carranza. Among them, only Carranza could claim above-average education, but he was older and his experienced network made him effective."

"Yes, Sombra, I can tell that the other two were effective despite their lack of education, mostly because of their deep insertion in their local and regional cultures."

"Precisely, Fierro, and those deep roots in their cultures, which made them such effective leaders of their neighbors, did not translate beyond the natural frontiers of their regionalism. Neither of them could have been effective leaders of a unified Mexico. This is why they did not make it."

"And Felipe Ángeles, Sombra, why did he not make it?"

"He may have been born not to be a leader, but to be a manager, Fierro. Perhaps Ángeles would have been a leader of a more educated México. At the time of the Mexican Revolution his knowledge was perceived as haughtiness. This is why he was frequently referred to as a 'professor' or a 'mathematician.' His foreign affiliations may have alienated him further. He had studied in France and had married a Californian lady with whom he had four children.[13] Zapata would recognize Ángeles's honorable nature, but would not go as far as trusting him; and cold, power-hungry Carranza was clever enough to see in Ángeles an obstacle to his dictatorial inclinations, and had him killed after a mock trial. Most sneakily, Carranza ordered a trial that would have Ángeles executed, but also issued a pardon as well, which he ordered be delivered after Ángeles execution."

[13] Slattery (1982, 18).

"What was the pardon for, Sombra?"

"Carranza was a sneaky despot, Fierro. He knew he was killing a hero and preferred Mexicans to believe he was unsuccessful in trying to save Ángeles's life than be seen as his executioner."

"I fear I cannot hold Spinoza down, listen to his neighing! *Ac proinde ignarus, et animo impotens non magis ex naturae jure tenetur, vitam sapienter instituere, quam aeger tenetur sano Corpore esse.*[14] Is this is how Carranza prevailed, Sombra?"

"That is it, Fierro."

"Did Mexicans waste an opportunity, Sombra?"

"I am not so sure they did, Fierro."

"Would they have worked more effectively under a leader with foreign overtones, Sombra?"

"Perhaps not, Fierro. Perhaps it was written from the early beginnings. After all, one of Ángeles's horses was named Ney, after the French Marshal Michel Ney, who was as apt at leading a cavalry attack as at retreating, as good at being cozy with the monarchy as with Napoleon."

"If Ángeles could not make up his mind, he could not lead, Sombra!"

"Precisely, Fierro. One should read more into symbols to predict the behavior of men. Felipe Ángeles may have castrated

One of Ángeles's horses was named Ney, after the French Marechal Michel Ney, who was as apt at leading a cavalry attack as a retreat, and was good at being as cozy with the monarchy as with Napoleon. One should read more into symbols to predict the behavior of men. Felipe Ángeles may have limited himself into becoming a half-foreigner in Mexico, but still had the guts to face his death, like Marechal Ney did, in commanding the firing squad in charge of his execution at Jardin de Luxembourg in 1815. Perhaps the Mexicans had sensed Ángeles's suicidal inclinations and chose not to follow him. Which brings up the last question, can any foreign-oriented aspiring leader ever be effective at leading local followers?

[14] "A man ignorant and weak of mind, is no more bound by natural law to order his life wisely, than a sick man is bound to be sound of body." Spinoza (1667, chapter I, paragraph 18). Translated in Spinoza (1883).

himself into becoming a half-foreigner, but he still had the guts to face his death. Like Marshal Ney did, in commanding the firing squad in charge of his execution at Jardin de Luxembourg in 1815."[15]

"Ney's execution was almost a suicide, Sombra! Like Ángeles's return to Mexico."

"Precisely, Fierro. Perhaps the Mexicans had sensed it and chose not to follow him. Which brings up the last question: Can any foreign-oriented aspiring leader ever be effective at leading local followers?"

"No, Sombra, and that is why Ángeles never became a leader of Mexicans. Perhaps later he would have been chosen to lead the subsidiary of a multinational, perhaps a soft drinks corporation."

"Fierro, that may be why his life was spared by the US government when they supported Huerta in getting rid of Madero."

[15] "Only when [Napoleon] began to totter France regained voice and action; and the long-suppressed protest, fanned by patriotic fears, broke out in betrayal and desertion. Marshal Ney, Prince de la Moskowa, who a year later was to rejoin Napoleon and suffer execution for it, when sent by him to the headquarters of the Allies in Paris, in the presence of the Tsar indulged in indiscreet and injudicious criticisms of Napoleon; but then it was new to him to be able to speak his mind" (Namier, 1958, 5).

# 11

# Contrasts with American Military Leadership: The Punitive Expedition

"Where do we go to now, Sombra?"

"Nowhere, Fierro. We will stay put."

"But is it not over, Sombra?"

"No, it never is. Americans invaded Mexico, Fierro."

"Fulfilling Ángeles's worst nightmare, Sombra?"

"Precisely, Fierro, and that invasion signaled the United States' preparation for entrance into World War I; it signaled the transition from cavalry to mechanized forces. Even airplanes were used in Mexico, to no avail, but they were used."

"The end of honor, Sombra?"

"Not at all, Fierro. We will gauge the supremacy of military academies and professional soldiers over spontaneous leadership."

"Where are the people, Sombra?"

"We will see how the US military establishment organized itself to generate first-class leaders despite responding to civilian command, Fierro."

"Still, Sombra, where are the people?"

"All right, there were people like General Patton."

"Why focus on him?"

"Because in many ways he was one of us, Fierro."

"Tell me more about Patton, Sombra."

"Perhaps I should start with his mentor, General Pershing, Fierro. If not with Jefferson and Hamilton."

West Point did not fulfill Jefferson's worst nightmares and did not become a new aristocracy; but it did become some sort of a caste, though a permeable one. Work is so hard, time so short, and demands so pressing, that, like most professionals, military men tend to mingle largely with themselves. Whole family traditions were built under the aegis of waging war. The Meigs and the Pattons are exemplary.

"Do that, Sombra."

"In a nutshell, Jefferson, the American Founding Father, would have had a much reduced army, Fierro, if any army at all. In fact, the US army was reduced to about one thousand men after independence."

"Near nothing for a country that size, Sombra."

"Precisely, Fierro. Though it was a smaller country then, Jefferson believed that patriotic ardor could be counted on repeatedly to build an army from scratch if it were necessary. But there were people like Alexander Hamilton who believed that though patriotic ardor was important, it was General Washington's strategic genius and the alliance with the French that did more to secure independence."

"So, Sombra?"

"Hamilton believed that war was a science that could be learned, Fierro.[1] That is how, two decades after independence, a small war college was created at West Point."

"How small was it, Sombra?"

"About four professors teaching how to build tunnels and trenches, Fierro. More of a school of engineering than a war college."

"Why so small, Sombra?"

"Fierro, the young American nation was worried that a large war college would end up generating an aristocratic military class inimical of the infant republic."[2]

"Did that happen, Sombra?"

"No, but much of the history taught today in the United States was shaped by cadets once taught at that academy."

[1] Federalist paper 25 (Schama, 2010, 61).

[2] Schama(2010, 66).

"Meaning that it might not be an aristocracy but it is some sort of a caste, Sombra?"

"Hard to tell, Fierro. But you see, work is so hard, time so short, and demands so pressing, that, like most professionals, military men tend to mingle largely with themselves. Whole family traditions were built under the aegis of waging war. The Meigs and the Pattons are exemplary."

"What has this got to do with Mexico, Sombra?"

"A lot, Fierro. The West Point graduates of 1915 are known as the class the stars fell on, on account of the unusually large share of graduates who attained the highest military ranking—but that could almost also be said of the classes of 1890 through 1915. George S. Patton graduated in 1909, and both Dwight D. Eisenhower and Omar Bradley in 1915."

"Were they exceptionally good or were they lucky to be around at the time of major conflicts?"

"A bit of both, Fierro, but still, they were relevant to Mexico."

"Meaning that what was happening in Mexico had direct bearing on what was being taught and discussed in classrooms at West Point, Sombra?"

"Precisely Fierro. Much of what happened in Central America and the Caribbean was churned by people graduated from that military academy."

"Like what, Sombra?"

"George W. Goethals graduated in 1880 and went on to be the chief engineer responsible for the building of the Panama Canal. General John J. Pershing graduated in 1886 and led the Punitive Expedition against Pancho Villa and later the American Expeditionary Force that took part in World War I."

"Punitive Expedition against our Villa, Sombra?"

"Yes, Pancho Villa, Fierro."

"Let us focus on Pershing, Sombra."

"So, Black Jack Pershing it will be, Fierro."

"Black Jack? Was he black, Sombra?"

"Not likely, Fierro. The first black American to graduate at West Point was of the class of 1877, but it would take another sixty-three years for a black graduate to become a general. Pershing had commanded a battalion of black men, hence his nickname."

"OK, let us focus on Villa-Pershing. Had not Villa been beaten down to nothing?"

"Not at all, Fierro. Villa remained strong in the North of Mexico, and he no longer had Ángeles to restrain him. Villa was embittered and blamed Americans for his military weakness."

"Why, Sombra?"

"Fierro, Villa was probably right. He complained that US tradesmen based in Columbus, New Mexico, had shortchanged him in a guns and ammunition deal and that the United States had allowed Carranza to attack him in November 1915 by way of railways over US soil. It doesn't really matter what happened, Fierro; the fact is that Villa sympathizers attacked the US city of Columbus in March 1916, and Americans responded with a ten-thousand-strong military incursion to hunt down Pancho Villa on Mexican soil."

"Wasn't that a bit of an overreaction, Sombra?"

"Perhaps not, Fierro, once you consider that the Punitive Expedition would prove a rehearsal for the American Expeditionary Force sent to Europe, under the same General Pershing's command."

"So, catching the Mexican hero was a useful pretext for Americans achieving preparedness for war, Sombra?"

"Well, let us not put it in such utilitarian terms, Fierro, after all, Columbus had been raided."

"Were the Americans successful, Sombra?"

"It depends how you qualify success, Fierro."

"Don't confuse me, Sombra, did they catch Pancho Villa?"

"Well, Fierro, that was what the US press demanded, but the Secretary of War knew it might not be possible, particularly if Villa took a train and sought refuge in Zapatista country."

> Pancho Villa's regional leadership had been boosted by the Punitive Expedition, which nonetheless had curbed his national effectiveness. Villa could have settled in a Republic of his own in Northern Mexico. American oil companies offered him precisely that, Fierro. They backed down when they realized he might not be able to deliver all the stability they aspired to. American oil companies did not really care who ran the place as long as they could pump the oil and ship it out; and it would remain like that for a long time.

"So what happened, Sombra?"

"The instruction General Pershing was issued was typically wishy-washy bureaucratic jargon, but it would be enough to curb the aggressiveness of Villa's forces."[3]

"What about respecting Mexico's sovereignty?"

"Good point, Fierro. That was a problem for the Americans, because if the Mexican people sided with Villa, which was to be expected, the Punitive Expedition would have to engage in the same slash-and-burn techniques they applied in Cuba and the Philippines, which naturally Carranza could not condone."

"So, they sent Pershing along in handcuffs, did they?"

"They did, Fierro, and with an unclear goal, too. Of course they did not catch Villa, not even after eleven months of pursuit."

"What? You mean that the Americans spent almost a year roaming around in Mexico, Sombra?"

"Yes, they did, Fierro."

"So? It was a failure, Sombra!"

"Not if you consider that Pershing was up against a lot."[4]

"What do you mean, Sombra?"

"Pancho Villa was a leader to the Mexicans, Fierro. Pershing's pursuit was like looking for a needle in a haystack, except that all the hay straws were against you, lying about where the needle was."[5]

"It doesn't surprise me at all, Sombra!"

"That is what happened, and that is why day after day Pershing's reports must have sounded like, 'I

> "Telling of the love for Pancho Villa were people like the peasant Pablo López, who, when caught, never renounced Villa and faced with a smile the Carrancista executioner's squadron that he, López himself, ordered to shoot, after requesting that he be not executed in the presence of any American!" Pablo López was greater than Marshal Ney, who knew he was entering history when he commanded his executioners to fire. López only demanded honor, recognition, on the spot. He may have been born an anonymous man, but he died a giant!

[3] Katz (1998, 568).

[4] "John's up against a lot," Funston told a newspaperman on the veranda of a San Antonio hotel (O'Connor, 1961, 119).

[5] Katz (1998, 570).

have the honor to inform you that Francisco Villa is everywhere and nowhere.' "[6]

"How far south did Pershing go?"

"Almost five hundred miles south before he decided to return, Fierro. It was a tough lesson."

"In what sense, Sombra?"

"Just think, Fierro; imagine the effort of supplying your cavalry."

"What with, Sombra?"

"Food, Fierro, food! They were not in the Argentine pampas but in arid Northern Mexico, for God's sake! At five hundred miles south of the border, their seven thousand horses and one hundred and fifty mules needed six tons of hay and nine tons of grain, day in and day out! Hungry horses 'chewed up leather bridles, saddlebags, halters, and ropes.' "[7]

"You are right, Sombra! It is too much to move from one place to another, unless you could do it by train."

"Which President Carranza would not allow, Fierro. Besides, Pershing's men needed women, too."

"How did the General sort that one out?"

"By running two sanitary brothels out of Columbus, Sombra! One for white Americans and another for black Americans.[8] Alcohol, drugs and gun smuggling was a big problem, too."[9]

"There was a lot of learning to be done, Sombra."

"Indeed, Fierro, including learning about military intelligence. Pershing appointed an officer to collect and analyze information gathered by natives."

"But, weren't the natives lying to Pershing, Sombra?"

"Of course they were, but that, too, had to be factored into the analysis, Fierro. By the end of 1916, Pershing was informing Washington of socialist revolutionary activities taking place in Northern Mexico.[10] His intelligence staff also came up with a wild plan to entrust Japanese agents to poison Villa."[11]

[6] Krauze (1998, 329).
[7] Welsome (2007, 185, 220).
[8] MacKell& Noel(2007, 235).
[9] Welsome (2007, 305).
[10] Talbert (2008, 7).
[11] Welsome (2007, 291).

"So, how did this rogue invasion end up, Sombra?"

"For a time the Americans retreated to the Northern frontier, on the Mexican side."

"But Sombra, that limited their effectiveness while becoming an increasingly uncomfortable thorn on the Mexican backside!"

"Precisely, Fierro. It could not last long, and eventually the Americans were called back."

"What about Pancho, Sombra?"

"Hard to say, Fierro. Pancho Villa had nearly four hundred men under his command when he raided Columbus. A year later he could be said to control Northern Mexico again with an army of several thousand. People like the peasant Pablo López, who, when caught, never renounced Villa and faced with a smile the Carrancista executioner's squadron that he, López himself, ordered to shoot, after requesting that he be not executed in the presence of any American!"[12]

"Very much like French Marshal Ney, Sombra!"

"Yes, but Pablo López was a peasant."

"So?"

"Pablo López had it in him, Fierro. He was not born to be a general; he was not educated. He only knew of oxen, cattle, mules and horses."

"Of course, but what are you trying to tell me, Sombra?"

"That Pablo López was greater than Marshal Ney, who knew he was entering history when he commanded his executioners to fire. López only demanded honor, recognition, on the spot. He may have been born an anonymous man, but he died a giant, Fierro!"

"I agree, I have always argued that peasants are the stuff of which heroes are made, Sombra!"

"Perhaps that is why Felipe Ángeles argued that Mexico needed someone who—like Uruguayan

Pancho Villa was killed in an ambush in 1923; like Emiliano Zapata before him, and like GumercindoSaraiva and Victoriano Lorenzo before them. They were all killed in ambushes at the hands of cowards hired by men who hide behind their desks and would never dare face the heroes. A facón would get rid of that type of men!

[12] Katz (1998, 576).

Zorrilla de San Martín did in Tabaré—would sing to Mexican Indians' epic struggle."[13]

"With or without a singer, it looks like with allegiances like those of Pablo López, Villa won, Sombra!"

"In that sense, win he did, Fierro; domestically at least because he again became a threat to Carranza, but internationally he had disenfranchised just about everybody, particularly in the United States. Nobody abroad spoke in Villa's favor; he had no future as a leader of Mexicans."

"Unless he could get rid of Carranza, Sombra."

"This was still too much for him, Fierro. Pancho Villa's regional leadership had been boosted by the Punitive Expedition, which nonetheless had curbed his national effectiveness."[14]

"He could have settled in a Republic of his own in Northern Mexico, Sombra."

"American oil companies offered him precisely that, Fierro. They backed down when they realized he might not be able to deliver all the stability they aspired to."[15]

"But they did not give up, did they, Sombra?"

"No, Fierro. They just wanted the oil, they did not really care who ran the place as long as they could pump the oil and ship it out, and it would remain like that for a long time."

"And Pancho?"

"He was killed in an ambush in 1923, Fierro."

"By the orders and the hands of cowards! Look at Spinoza, Sombra! Look at him, he is so sad he cannot even neigh!"

"I wonder what type of men issue those orders, Fierro."

"People who hide behind their desks, Sombra! Those types of people, a facón would get rid of them!"

"Well, this was meant to be about Patton and Pershing, wasn't it, Fierro?"

"Yes, but let us not forget Pancho, Sombra. He died at the transition."

"Which transition, Fierro?"

[13] Gilly(2008, 282); Zorrila de San Martín (1960).

[14] Katz (1998, 613).

[15] Katz (1998, 667).

"From when men would fight armed with courage to when wars would be fought by professionals, Sombra."

"Nonsense, Fierro. These professionals needed courage, too. Besides, I am more interested in how the modern army would accept and apply innovation. Horses are doomed, Fierro."

"What will you replace them with, Sombra?"

"Tanks and airplanes, Fierro."

"Nonsense, you saw how all nine Pershing planes failed—all of them, Sombra."

"True, Fierro, they failed here, when airplane flying was barely fifteen years old and run by faulty ninety-horsepower engines. But still, Pershing had nine-times-ninety horses flying in reconnaissance missions."

"You'd have to be mad to mount any of those horses, Sombra!"

"Precisely, Fierro, this is why I am interested; this modern army would accept some degree of madness, despite its insistence on obedience. Somehow these West Point men were trained to try, to experiment—besides obedience."

"Who did it, Sombra? I am not an organization man. I am interested in who did it."

"Fierro, take Captain Benjamin Foulois, for example."

"Who was he?"

"He was America's entire Air Force at the time. He disassembled his nine Curtiss planes and shipped them on a train to Columbus, New Mexico, guarded by riflemen. Reassembled them upon arrival and served as best he could."

"But he failed, Sombra!"

"The planes did; neither he nor his pilots failed, Fierro."

"Who was he, Sombra?"

> One of the more interesting sides of West Point is that it was initiated by engineering professors. This is how their army stayed modern; accepting and applying innovation. Horses were superseded by cars and airplanes. All nine planes deployed in the Punitive Expedition failed. But then, heavier-than-air flying machines were barely fifteen years old and were powered by faulty ninety horse power engines. Some madness was necessary to man those airplanes, but the interesting thing is that this modern army would accept some degree of madness, despite its insistence on obedience. Somehow these West Point men were trained to try, to experiment.

"A birdwatcher, Fierro. That's how he got into it!"

"A birdwatcher! We are talking of war here!"

"We are talking of flying, Fierro! This man began by bird-watching but had to make a living and joined his father's plumbing company; but curiously restless as he was, he joined the army and he fought many battles with Pershing."

"So, Pershing again, and this was his pal."

"Yes, and he was seasoned, too, Fierro. Upon his return, Foulois experimented with dirigibles and aviation. He wrote an academic paper suggesting that airplanes would be helpful in reconnaissance and that it would be possible to communicate between them and staff on land."

"Wild, Sombra, wild!"

"That is what is marvelous, Fierro; wild as it was, the paper caught the eye of the army's chief signal officer who supported him in his experiments."

"Only experiments, Sombra!"

"But six years after the Wright brothers' maiden flight, this man flew a Wright plane for forty minutes, Fierro![16] Captain Foulois was experimenting, yes, but at the onset of a new era. Somehow he envisioned it and somehow these West Point guys encouraged him to persevere. That is what I think is admirable at West Point as an organization, military or not."

"Yes, but ..."

"No buts, Fierro! If these guys were all like you they would have never dismounted! Learn from them!"

"OK, Sombra, but organizations are made of men. Who was Patton?"

"Quite an extraordinary man, Fierro."

"In what sense?"

"I would say in most senses that matter, Fierro."

"Good fighter, Sombra?"

"Excellent, in the sense he was admired by his men and feared by the enemy, Fierro."

"That's good. A good fighter should always scare the hell out of the enemy. Tell me more, Sombra."

[16] Welsome (2007, 171).

"He came of a lineage of Southern military men. When the South lost the Civil War, Fierro, the family did not want to hear of reconstruction and moved to California. There the widow remarried and this George Patton, the one that fought with General Pershing, came into being, from that root."

"So far nothing extraordinary, Sombra."

"Because he was small at first, Fierro. That's when his enemies should have gotten rid of him. It became impossible later."

"That much, Sombra?"

"Listen Fierro, the man had family money and married into even more money, northern textile manufacturers, that helped him have a dozen horses and play polo, but that does not explain why he would compete in the Olympics Pentathlon in 1912."

"Did he win?"

"No, Fierro, as a matter of fact he came in fifth place. But would physical conditioning be any more important than acumen and knowledge in leading people to win a battle?"

"Well, what did Patton have going for him then?"

"Fierro, to start with, he had foresight and perseverance."

"Shown how, Sombra?"

"For instance, Patton's length of service would not entitle him to aspire to replace General Pershing's aide-de-camp when the latter went ill and could not make it to the Punitive Expedition."

"Why did Patton want to join in the first place?"

"Because he was a soldier, Fierro, and that was the only battle opportunity he could have."

"So?"

"So he offered himself to General Pershing."

"Who accepted him?"

"Not immediately, Fierro. Pershing asked Patton why he should take him rather than the hordes that wanted that position."

"So, why should he?"

"Patton answered that Pershing should take him because nobody wanted it as badly as he did!"

"Hmm, that's a persuasive argument, if it later can be backed by deeds. And what did Pershing say?"

"He told him to pack and be ready, Fierro. Patton replied that he had already packed and was ready. 'I'll be dammed,' General Pershing replied.

So there, Patton backed it up with deeds on the spot, Sombra!"

"Yes he did, and that was Patton's first step into war. He jumped into war just like we jumped into herding cattle, Fierro. I would not ask for permission when I thought I should go with a group of gauchos, and I taught Fabio Cáceres to do the same, to follow his instincts."[17]

"Did Patton know what he was getting into, Sombra?"

"At least he thought he did, Fierro. Patton saw himself as a reincarnation of great historical warriors."

"What?"

"As you hear it, Fierro."

"So, he believed he was prone to greatness and sought to position himself accordingly, Sombra?"

"Probably, Fierro."

"How did Patton fare in Pershing's Punitive Expedition, Sombra?"

"He must have done well, Fierro, because Pershing took Patton with him on America's Expeditionary Force in Europe."

"Any particular recollection of his actions in Mexico?"

"Well, Fierro, Patton hunted down a couple of Villa's fighters whom he transported back to camp, dead, tied down like deer onto his car's engine."

"Rather brutish of him, Sombra."

"Not particularly wholesome, I must admit, Fierro."

> Patton was a good father. He taught his son how to hunt and fish; he would pull the child out of class if he thought the boy was missing out on something more worthy. One day he pulled his son out of school to attend a lecture by T.E. Lawrence, the famed Lawrence of Arabia, because Patton believed in exposing his son to the greatness in great men.

"Why do you think he did it, Sombra?"

"He must have been contemptuous of the enemy, Fierro. He was known to enjoy killing enemy soldiers because he believed them to be agents of evil."[18]

[17] "Cuando yo tenía tu edad, le hacía el gusto al cuerpo sin pedir licencia a naides."Freely translated as: "When I was your age I would follow my body's wish without anybody's permission" (Güiraldes, 1926, chapter 5).

[18] Hanson (1999, 273).

"Killing is one thing, Sombra. Parading the corpses of the dead is quite another!"

"Vehicle design did not help, Fierro. These were passenger cars; Patton called the event America's first motorized war incursion."

"Not much to be proud of, Sombra!"

"I agree, but then, when it comes to war, there is little to be unremorsely proud of."

"Tell me more about this man, Sombra."

"He was definitely a man of contrasting qualities, Fierro."

"I want you to describe him as if I were in need of recognizing him on the street, Sombra!"

"Given your own story, Fierro, should we not start by Patton's role as a father?"

"What about that, Sombra?"

"He cannot have been a bad father, Fierro."

"Why not, Sombra?"

"He taught his son how to hunt and fish; he would pull him out of class if he thought the boy was missing out on something more worthy."[19]

"Like what, Sombra?"

"For instance, Fierro, one day he pulled his son out of school to attend a lecture by T. E. Lawrence, the famed Lawrence of Arabia."[20]

"Why did Patton Senior do that?"

"Because he believed in exposing his son to the greatness in great men, Fierro!"[21]

"Not bad, Sombra!"

"He was definitely much loved by his daughter, too, who would recall him as the easiest weeper!"[22]

"Could Patton be a weeping General, Sombra?"

"Fierro, Patton was a romantic elitist. He would quickly rise to anger but was also sentimental. He would weep when being read literature by his family."[23]

[19] Sobel (1997, 21).
[20] Sobel (1997, 15).
[21] Sobel (1997, 17).
[22] Sobel (1997, 7).
[23] Sobel (1997, 7).

> Patton believed that a leader inspires even in his details. He admired Pershing for shaving every day during the Punitive Expedition in Mexico.
>
> If winning is not the purpose but the means, and the purpose begs the foundation of respect on which to build a democratic society, shaving may not be all, but it shows the way forward.

"Could he not read, like me, Sombra?"

"With difficulty, Fierro. Patton was dyslexic."

"That would be hard to diagnose in me, Sombra!"

"And unfortunately in a significant share of our population, Fierro!"

"So, Patton's family would take turns in making him weep, what else, Sombra?"

"He would practice lectures and stern looks in his mirror, Fierro."

"What for, Sombra?"

"Patton believed that a leader inspires even in his details. He admired Pershing for shaving every day during the Punitive Expedition in Mexico."[24]

> Patton rehearsed grimaces to a mirror because he believed that motivating men into battle required that a hardened warring leader capable of inspiring them to face death despite the leader being very much like them.
>
> Patton was a man with many dimensions. His elitism, his blindness except for targets, must have made him terribly impatient with those he was persuaded were not up to it and may even have undermined the morale of the rest. Perhaps that is why he slapped a subordinate in Italy, jeopardizing his own career.

"Villa did not shave much, Sombra, and he was a leader to his men."

"True, Fierro, I think it also depends on where you want to lead."

"In what sense, Sombra?"

"Well, Fierro, if you have not much of a purpose besides winning, what to shave for?"

"So?"

"Yet if winning is not the purpose but the means, and the purpose begs the foundation of respect on which to build a democratic society, shaving may not be all, but it shows the way forward."

"Oh nonsense, Sombra!"

"Perhaps, but I would rather be led by those who shave and wash, Fierro."

[24] Klan (2006, 50–51).

"Sure, and by those who make grimaces to a mirror, too, Sombra?"

"The grimaces into a mirror are a different matter altogether, Fierro. Apparently Patton believed that motivating men into battle required that a hardened warring leader inspire them to face death despite the leader being very much like them."[25]

"But if he was so effective because he understood soldiers so well, why would he need to slap them around?"

"Patton was a man with many dimensions. His elitism, his blindness except for targets, must have made him terribly impatient with those he was persuaded were not up to task and may even undermine the morale of the rest. Fierro, you and I have fought, and despite our bravery we both know that at times we were not up to it."

"But we fought, Sombra! Did we not?"

"We sure did, Fierro, we had to."

"Unless we were given the chance to rest on the efforts of others, Sombra? Is that what you mean? Let others risk their lives for us? Like Patton, I would slap those out of this world if necessary."

"Well, Fierro, I think that is what he did. Unfortunately, he was misinterpreted and perhaps the case was blown out of proportion by those who were not exposed to the same crises as fighters."

"The cowards never let him off the hook, did they?"

Patton was a cavalry man, but in Europe the allies had reached a stale-mate. Both forces were deeply entrenched and none could advance on the other unprotected, like on horseback. Patton saw the allies' first attempts at armored cars and saw the future of army attacks in them. Despite a life on horseback, whether fighting or for pleasure and sport, Patton gave up on horses and saw that putting armor around an engine on wheels would play the trick. Patton asked to be appointed head of a force which did not yet exist in the American army.

He was a romantic and saw in armored cars the weapon which would define future battles.

The first tanks were adaptations of agricultural machinery. They were slow. Infantrymen would walk alongside or behind the tanks, protected from light fire by the tanks which would have a cannon or a machine gun installed.

[25] Sobel (1997, 8). French General De Gaulle was not much easier to get close to. He believed that familiarity breeds contempt, as in "no man is a hero to his valet" (De Gaulle, 1960, 58).

"Never, Fierro. Many years later, while on a home visit during World War II, Patton was visiting a military hospital, and while accompanied by medical staff and journalists he turned upon the latter and yelled at them that he knew they were expecting him to slap another soldier. He left the room and took refuge in a larger ward where he pulled out a handkerchief and wept into it."[26]

"Moving, Sombra, moving. It is very sad to see the loneliness of true men in the hands of the common cowardly ones.[27] But what was so great in Patton, Sombra?"

"Fierro, Patton was great in many ways, not least among them in his disinterested visionary stance."

"How so?"

"When with Pershing and the Expeditionary Force in Paris, Patton saw the Allies' first attempts at armored cars and saw the future of army attacks in them, although he was a cavalryman."

"He gave up on horses then, Sombra?"

"Yes, he did, Fierro."

"Why?"

"Fierro, the Allies had reached a stalemate. Both forces were deeply entrenched and neither could advance on the other unprotected like on horseback."

"So, putting armor around an engine would play the trick?"

"They thought it would, Fierro. This is why they called those contraptions a tank. Prototypes looked like an upside-down tank."[28]

Absentee fathers are a major handicap Latin America must face. After all, offspring had little presence in Fierro and Sombras's life, very much like Pedro Páramo had little bearing on Luciano Preciado's. All the way from Argentina to Mexico it is the same; including *Love in the Time of Cholera*, where Florentino Ariza is shaped on Gabriel García Marquez's elusive father. How can we hope to educate, to instill self-esteem in our people, if fathers abandon their children?

[26] Sobel (1997, 9).

[27] Organizations have long memories. Dealing with soldiers that can no longer fight has haunted the US Army to the point that still today the US president does not send condolence letters to the families of those who committed suicide while on duty, though he does if a soldier dies falling off a jeep (Dreazen, 2009).

[28] Small, Westwell and Westwood (2002, 862).

"What about the moving aspect of it, Sombra? At least horses are fast!"

"The first tanks were adaptations of agricultural machinery. Indeed they were slow. Infantrymen would walk alongside or behind the tanks, protected from light fire by the tanks, which would have a cannon or a machine gun installed."

"Were they effective, Sombra?"

"At first they were not, Fierro. But tanks became faster, easier to maneuver, more effective to shoot from. Ultimately no army would do without them, but it took a lot of work to make them effective and that was partly because of Patton."

"In what sense was Patton involved, Sombra?"

"In all senses, Fierro. Having seen the opportunity, Patton dropped horses altogether and asked to be appointed head of a force that did not yet exist in the US army."

"A gambler, too, was he?"

"He did not need the money, Fierro. He was a romantic and saw in armored cars the weapon that would define future battles."

"What did he do about it, Sombra?"

"Fierro, Patton worked earnestly at supporting the development of more effective armored cars and ultimately became commander of the force."

"Did he actually put his hands to it, Sombra?"

"He did, Fierro; his children recollect him working after dinner with a tank engineer developing better suspension for the armored vehicles."[29]

"What came out of all this vision, renouncement of cavalry and heroism, Sombra?"

> In the process, leaders like Gumercindo and Garibaldi and the rest took care of their followers as generously as possible; for it is not possible to lead effectively unless you can persuade the followers that you are not in it for yourself. The litmus test is whether you are willing to put your life, or career, at stake for the cause you ask your followers to put theirs at stake; leading from the front proves it.

[29] Sobel (1977, 14).

"Fierro, Patton and his force were deployed to North Africa where he beat the hell out of the Nazis. He subsequently helped take Sicily and marched up North through Italy."

"He sounds like a fighter all right, but what was so special about him, Sombra?"

"Fierro, perhaps there is nothing more important about him than that he held his soldiers in his highest esteem, to the point they became devoted to him—which turned them into an implacable force, in effect the most feared by the enemy."[30]

"Was there a downside to this man, Sombra?"

"As with many great men, there were great downsides to this one, too."

"Such as, Sombra?"

"He was known to unrepentantly profess racist remarks, particularly about Jews and blacks."[31]

"That was cheap of him, Sombra. My Spinoza is getting restless!"

"I agree, Fierro. A sad side of an otherwise great man."

"What happened to him at last, Sombra?"

"He died in a car crash, Fierro, at the close of the war."

"A rather inglorious way of dying for a man that lived to fight. Wouldn't you say so, Sombra?"

"So unlike Patton that perhaps it was no accident, Fierro."[32]

"Are you suggesting Patton may have been killed, Sombra?"

"It will be argued, Fierro. But perhaps it is a people's natural reaction to deny the death of the hero, like in Gumercindo's case, remember?"

"Yes, Sombra, it is most sad that heroes like Gumercindo, Victoriano Lorenzo, Ángeles, Villa, Zapata, and Patton die either at the hands or in the mouths of cowards who would never have been up to their feats."

[30] Goffee and Jones (2006, 154).

[31] D'Este (1995, 172; 1995, 172); Alexander (2005, 231).

[32] Wilcox (2010).

## Lessons from the Punitive Expedition

"We have seen a lot, Fierro. We have focused on the differences and more recently on the similarities of these men."

"Indeed, Sombra. I liked that Patton, a good father too."

"Glad you noticed that, Fierro. For absentee fathers is a major handicap we have. After all, we have had little presence in their lives, very much like Pedro Páramo had little bearing on Luciano Preciado's life. All the way from Argentina to Mexico it is the same. How can we hope to educate, to instill self-esteem in our people, if fathers abandon their children?"

"Why was Patton different, Sombra?"

"We haven't figured out that one yet, but he shows that it is possible to be a hero and a father, to focus on the large and the small things at the same time."

"Again, I liked that Patton, Sombra."

"Precisely. This is to say that the fact that we, most Latin Americans, are different from North Americans does not mean that all American Scientific Management techniques should be discarded altogether."

"I see your point, Sombra."

"Technology may neutralize bravery, Fierro, like the cannon once did, and the tank and the airplanes did later."

"True, Sombra, but Patton was no coward, however much he may have embraced technology!"

"Granted, Fierro, but what we need is to develop the independence of thought that will help us choose what techniques and styles are relevant to us and to develop the ones that are lacking."

"Is that all, Sombra?"

"No, there is more, Fierro. Patton was not alone, he was the outcome of an organization which, though committed to discipline and obedience, would not frown upon innovation."

"Yes, let's ride back, Sombra."

"Don't you want to know more, Fierro?"

"No, Sombra, I've had enough. One needs to recognize when more information will not add as much as putting to good use that which we have already acquired. There is no more time to waste, let's ride back and do what needs to be done."

"Gallop for it, Fierro!" And as Fierro eagerly spurred Spinoza, the latter neighs: "*Hominesnamque non utsunt, seduteosdemessevellent, concipiunt; unde factum est.*"[33]

[33] "For they [philosophers] conceive of men not as they are but as they themselves would like them to be" (Spinoza, 1667, chapter 1, introduction) translated as (Spinoza, 1883, chapter 1, introduction).

# 12

# Epilogue

Leadership is about life, and yet too many workplaces are about the living dead. At living dead workplaces, people are sapped of their energy, of their will, of their desire to become; there, all creativity is beaten off them until mediocrity is instilled through conformity. This is why I called such places saladeros, places where people jerked beef while they unwittingly salted themselves out of life. The preserving technology may have changed, but the slow-kill process has not.

> At saladeros people are sapped of their energy, of their will, of their desire to become; there, all creativity is beaten off them until mediocrity is installed through conformity. This is why I have called such places saladeros, places where people jerked beef while they unwittingly salted themselves out of life in the process. The preserving technology may have changed, but the slow kill process has not.

I contrasted the saladeros with the unbounded freedom of two gauchos, Fierro and Sombra, who roam across the continent drawing leadership and management lessons from popular revolts. I chose revolts because they can be viewed as organizations, and I chose mostly nineteenth- and early twentieth-century revolts because they preceded American Scientific Management and thus showed how Latin Americans used to manage themselves before business schools and multinationals set foot in the region and required conformity to foreign management techniques mostly designed by observing foreigners, not Latin Americans.

> Subsidiaries are foreign in that investment decisions, including those pertaining to innovation or strategy, are mostly made abroad, excluding local managers from the challenges that might allow them to develop to their full leadership potential. The result is stunted bosses who offer poor inspiration for younger, upcoming managers. The arrangement produces foot-dragging and cynicism among followers, who remain deprived of a learning process that could generate authentic leadership rather than conformity to an inglorious, slow and long death.

Not all is wrong with the management by multinationals, except that, for all the modern talk about adopting local physiognomy, their subsidiaries remain foreign. They are foreign in that their investment decisions, including those pertaining to innovation or strategy, are mostly made abroad, excluding local managers from the challenges that might allow them to develop to their full leadership potential. The result is ineffective bosses who offer poor inspiration for younger, upcoming managers. The arrangement produces foot-dragging and cynicism among followers, who remain deprived of a learning process that could generate authentic leadership rather than conformity to an inglorious, slow, and long death.

Popular revolts, despite the killing orgies, were live theaters where followers were drawn to their peak performance at a young age and where leaders were quickly separated from the chaff. These were times where conversion meant not exchanging currencies but adherence to causes worthy of our lives; where transcendence meant seeking justice, not owning the latest model of an electronic gadget.

From that world of revolts, of men and women larger than themselves, I drew cases that might not fit into Harvard Business School case style of teaching, but which we have a lot to learn from if we are to show the path to aspiring leaders of our people. There may well be more and better cases than the ones I have selected, but these sufficed to make my points.

In the first place, popular revolts offer the stage to make evident that true, authentic leadership is for everyone, at all organizational levels. We can all be leaders to some, at some instance. It requires the disposition to grab it and run with it.

Humble peasants—like Gumercindo Saraiva, Pancho Villa and Emiliano Zapata—turned themselves into leaders of thousands while barely articulate, let alone literate. Gumercindo does not seem to have been an extrovert either; he was withdrawn, but his rectitude and determination left no doubt as to what he stood for. Even his heavy-handed disciplinary actions were taken as evidence of his fairness and transparency of his objectives. Like Gumercindo, Giuseppe (Joseph) Garibaldi lived for a cause for which he ultimately died, after fighting for it on three continents. In the process, leaders like Gumercindo and Garibaldi, and the rest, took care of their followers as generously as possible; for it is not possible to lead effectively unless you can persuade the followers that you are not in it only for yourself. The true test is whether you are willing to put your life, or your career, at stake for the cause to which you ask your followers to dedicate theirs. Leading from the front is the proof.

These leaders were no Franz Humer, Roche Pharmaceutical's CEO, managing the stage of his performance when being interviewed by a business school professor, making him wait for a long minute before replying to his question.[1] Take the Mexican peasant López, for instance. When facing the Mexican firing squad that would ultimately shoot his life out of him, he ordered all Americans off the scene, then took command of the firing squad and ordered them to shoot.

> There are lessons to be drawn from those lives, however humble in origins, as well as from their deaths. The main lesson is that, to have effective leadership, authenticity may not be all, but it surely is an essential attribute.

Peasant López had been caught and had reached the end of his line, but it was not up to the enemy to deprive him of his life; he would leave on his own terms. López behaved very much like the French Marshal Ney whom Felipe Ángeles honored by naming his horse after him.

Peasant López knew that his role in the world was greater than the life he was ending—again, like Felipe Ángeles. These were

[1] Goffee and Jones (2006, 40).

men had situation-sensing skills, similar to those of Roche's Mr. Humer, but they were not on stage; or rather, life was their stage, for their lives were at stake.

There are lessons to be drawn from those lives, however humble in origin, as well as from their deaths. The main lesson is that, to achieve effective leadership, authenticity may not be all, but it surely is an essential attribute.

Juan Vicente Gómez was a similarly styled leader. Like Gumercindo, he was reserved, loyal and trustworthy; initially, he was a bean counter for the charismatic Cipriano Castro, the extroverted Venezuelan leader. Yet it was Gómez who prevailed, despite his reserved nature. There was no vociferous ordering in Gómez, no exalted speeches. Once triumphant, he left Cipriano Castro in command in Caracas and set off to lead his people in the pacification of Venezuela. It took him a few years more of fighting but he eventually prevailed and cast a shadow over Cipriano Castro to the point that Gómez ended up replacing Castro. Much can be held against Gómez, but to a large extent, much of what is positive in Venezuela today is owed to the developmental environment that Gómez's pacification campaign made possible.

Like Gumercindo and Garibaldi, Gómez was also a bit of a foreigner to the country he would subsequently stabilize through his Andino followers. This brings the followers to stage, through the recruitment these leaders emphasized.

> Popular revolts, despite the killing orgies, were live theaters where followers were drawn to their peak performance at a young age and where leaders were quickly separated from the chaff. These were times where conversion meant not exchanging currencies but adherence to causes worthy of our lives; where transcendence meant seeking justice, not owning the latest model of an electronic gadget.

The effectiveness of all the leaders portrayed lay in the mutual loyalty rapport they established with their followers. This is not management to be learned, but to be practiced. The leaders' effectiveness lay in that their followers were all in-groups. The out-groups were bought out, defected or were suppressed. This may seem a very non-corporate way of managing business, but it surely is a truthful one, one in which everyone knows when they are wanted. There is no doubt about it, followers feel wanted or they would not be there. This is the atmosphere that rules in start-ups, when each employee is an in-group member and perhaps even an out-group hater. On the other hand, much of the corporate world today seems to rejoice in keeping people under the gun, making them wonder whether they will be the next one to be shot out.

Popular revolts may start small, like start-ups, but may quickly grow to the thousands and retain similar cohesiveness. They grow providing their message fits a need and the recruiters, backed by a truthful leader, sense there is a purpose worthy of their joining. This is why Gumercindo recruited in the hinterland. That was where his conservative message better matched the anxiety prevailing in a Brazil that had recently done away with slavery and become a republic.

Recruiting where the corporate message fits the desires of the would-be recruits is a lesson many corporate recruiters at foreign subsidiaries have missed. Attempting to match the profile of recruits at headquarters' subsidiaries, recruiters often target the local top schools, luring the young winners who have survived the toughest war they could face at their stage in life: honorably graduating the top schools of their cities.

> Crowds are responsive to a militant core, they need direction, and they seek direction. A militant core may provide the guidance, but the rest do not feel disenfranchised. The secret of this success is that these revolutionary leaders recruited geographically. Their followers were bound by webs of loyalty that preceded their joining the organization. The leaders recruited teams, not individuals. If the people they recruited were not family related, they at least were friends or neighbors. When they moved forward they were families at war.

Yet the only work the subsidiaries have to offer is that of the saladeros, more fit for the already dead and the dying. Unsurprisingly, turnover is high. Subsidiaries should be recruiting at the lesser schools, where what they have to offer is a bonus to those who—like gladiators—have toiled under the most adverse of conditions. Skills at the lesser schools may be in shorter supply, or may be lacking altogether—like proficiency at foreign languages, and perhaps finesse—but all can be part of on-the-job training. Perhaps this is what makes great the Brazilian bank Bradesco. This bank focuses its recruitment at the lower echelons of society and then nurtures its workforce into a level of effectiveness and a sense of belonging that to many a foreign banker, as I have heard more than one say, Bradesco seems more like a sect than a bank.

Surely, recruiting where the message is aligned with the leader and has a better fit with the environment should render a more cohesive workforce faster and with less attrition. But it does not explain why anyone would drop what he or she is doing and choose to put his or her life at stake by joining a popular revolt that will take them thousands of miles away from home. That needs further explanation, because large, popular revolts are still small in proportion to the size of the population they ultimately need to manage if they are to be successful—as Gómez was in Venezuela or Saraiva was in Brazil.

> In Latin America, as in all more collectivist cultures, people need to know a lot more about the other than in North America to develop the level of trust that is common currency in the United States and which encourages faster cohesiveness among teams there.

This is when the Canetti concept of crowd comes in handy. Crowds are responsive to a militant core, they need direction, and they seek direction. A militant core may provide the guidance, but the rest do not feel disenfranchised. The secret of this success is that these revolutionary leaders recruited geographically. Their followers were bound by webs of loyalty that preceded their joining the organization. The leaders recruited teams, not individuals. If the people they recruited were not family related, they at least were friends or neighbors. When they moved forward they were families at war.

Even an outright libertarian like Garibaldi worked mostly with Italians. The defenders of the city of Montevideo organized themselves into legions by nationalities. Garibaldi fought with Italians. Gumercindo with Maragatos and men of the Pampas, Gómez fought mostly with Andinos, Pancho Villa with northern Mexicans, and Emiliano Zapata with southern Mexicans. This suggests that their strength may have been thwarted by not seeking recruits farther than their own turf for the competencies their organizations lacked. That is possible. Oribe failed at the siege of Montevideo precisely because he could not block the city from being supplied by sea. Oribe fought only on land. This is where Garibaldi's response to the lack of local competencies is so illuminating.

When fighting in Brazil, Garibaldi needed armed boats and he had them built. He brought Italian carpenters from Montevideo into Brazil and used the talents of an American, John Griggs, to build the ships to fight Brazil's Imperial Navy on the sea. Garibaldi still stuck to Italians, but he sought them wherever they were. Castro and Gómez initially fought with spears, machetes and old Mouser rifles, but they would seize the weapons—and the talent to operate them—as their less cohesive adversaries dispersed, leaving their guns behind. Pancho Villa welcomed the organizational, strategic, and artillery competencies of the outsider General Felipe Ángeles to fight the war against General Huerta.

But by and large, all these leaders fought with armies that were entirely in-groups; they were teams before they joined the organizations, very much like Brazilian samba schools operate to render a world-class show. But his is not limited to Latin America. In India, one can find similar organizational arrangements, like among the dabbawalas of Mumbai or the Indian traders who took over Belgium's diamond business in Antwerp, recruiting out of Palanpur in the state of Gujarat.

Out-groups today are a business school phenomenon, offshoots of a recruiting strategy that works more poorly in Latin America: hiring individuals from the market and then training them to work as teams. Some become in-group members, others are left out. In Latin America, as in all more collectivist cultures, people need to know a lot more about the other than in North America to develop the level of trust that is common currency in the United States and which encourages faster cohesiveness among teams there.

> In Latin America, the lesson learned from the leaders of popular revolts is that they sought teams first and then looked for the skills within them, or like Garibaldi, brought teams from outside to fill out the competencies gaps.

The leaders I portrayed here all recruited among or through people they knew—not the common fare taught at business schools, where this may even sound like a crippling strategy. In the world of business schools, high-performing teams are set up with an eye on skills more readily than on compatibility of the members.[2] But this is a lesson derived from northern business schools, which deal with individuals who can team up rapidly to jointly make the best of their skills. In Latin America, the lesson learned from the leaders of popular revolts is that they sought teams first and then looked for the skills within them, or like Garibaldi, brought teams from outside to fill the competencies gaps.

It is worth thinking of ways to emulate this, such as hiring through referrals or asking your collaborators to recommend someone to fill an opening, rather than advertising for the best holder of the skill and expecting him or her to join an existing team. Skeptics might argue that revolt leaders made constrained decisions and had to work with what came their way. I argue that all organizations must make constrained decisions and that this decision making is not valid only at war, for it is also the strength of Brazil's samba schools, which recruit in their neighborhoods and deliver world-class entertainment for almost no pay. At war or for fun, closely knit Latin American teams precede the winning organization, and those that choose to ignore this fact are likely to spend more resources to achieve similar results, or even succumb.

> Transcendental experiences at war, which in any case are relatively recent, may have helped generate present-oriented societies, at least in terms of gratification, but it does mean that people nurtured in this ethos will have little patience with the year-long performance evaluation cycle deeply engrained in so many multinationals. Giving people too little or too late—like when excluding worker's parents from medical insurance—amounts to giving them less than they need and expect; it is not a wise people-management policy but it seems to have been unthinkingly rolled out by multinationals in Latin America.

[2] Katzenbach and Smith (2005, 118).

The leaders I portrayed fought for a cause. The cause was mostly for restoring order, as in Venezuela's Marcha Restauradora, Gumercindo's restoration of an Empire, or Villa-Zapata-Carranza's struggle to restore the democratic pact that Huertas had broken. When people fight for a cause they demand little pay, or they defer payment. Sometimes they defer payment for years, as in Garibaldi's defense of Montevideo, Gumercindo's Federalist Revolt or Castro-Gómez's six-year exile in Colombia prior to the victorious Marcha Restauradora through Venezuela.

When it comes to deferring payment for years and putting up with the risk of dying at war, one can safely say that payment was not a highly important motivator, at least to those people under those circumstances. Then what was important, besides a cause, a vision, which the leaders were mostly at a loss to articulate?

Recognition was vastly important; and in an environment where one might not be alive the next day, recognition there and then was the only legitimate way to give it and get it. This is largely why these makeshift armies had so many officers, because promotions were cheap to distribute in that they carried no salary increase. It may seem like an expedient solution, but it worked.

We are dealing with symbolic compensation here. This may involve small gestures showing the leader cares, like Garibaldi's in offering his own shirt to a soldier without one. It may carry the weight of a pension for the mother of Juan Santamaría, who gave his life for Costa Rica, but the people who offer their lives expect at least

> Being born of an original sin has a cost. A century later, Panama still has not managed to fulfill a modern nation's mandate. Its leaders are unsure of the merit of their rights and at the end of the last century, during the abduction of General Noriega, they were still seen seeking verification of their rights at the guichet of the power that created them. That is what happens when the elite does not feel responsible for building a nation because they have not earned it. It is the same with corporations. You cannot expect to effectively run a corporation with people who have been disenfranchised from it. There will be a lot of foot dragging. This is why the authenticity of the leader, expressed in his deeds and alignment with his utterances, is crucial to effective followership.

recognition for it. And if a society has been made out of these men and women, it is quite likely that immediate and generous recognition goes a long way in securing alliances and supreme efforts, for tomorrow we may all be dead.

These transcendental experiences at war, which are relatively recent, may have helped generate present-oriented societies, at least in terms of gratification,[3] but it does mean that people nurtured in this ethos will have little patience with the year-long performance evaluation cycle deeply engrained in so many multinationals. Giving people too little or too late—like when excluding worker's parents from medical insurance—amounts to giving them less than they need and expect; it is not a wise people-management policy but it seems to have been unthinkingly rolled out by multinationals in Latin America.

When managing Latin Americans it would make much better sense to provide feedback on the spot and to reward upon deed rather than to fit gratifications into a yearly budget cycle, having bonuses distributed by managers who, being present oriented themselves, are likely to make poor assessments of anything beyond the worker's behavior over the most recent few weeks.

Perhaps a sign of the times, personal honor has become a fuzzy concept; but it still carries enormous weight in Latin America. This is why the topic of Panama's independence still meets tongue-in-cheek responses from Latin Americans. Not because Panamanians did not deserve independence, but because of the way they achieved it, by treason. Essentially, the leaders of the Panamanian secession from Colombia reaped the opportunity of moneyed US support and bribed those who would have second thoughts. Then they made themselves president, cabinet ministers, and so forth. They later had statues built of themselves, and their descendants make sure they are still revered—for not insisting on it might open a lot of painful questions.

But being born of an original sin has a cost. A century later, Panama still has not managed to fulfill a modern nation's mandate. Its leaders are unsure of the merit of their rights and at the end of the last century, during the abduction of General Noriega, they were still seen seeking verification of their rights at the *guichet*

[3] Samovar, Porter and McDaniel (2009, 212).

of the power that created them. In the meantime, they could not be bothered to put nameplates on the streets of their capital city, nor numbers on the houses along them. There still is no residential distribution of correspondence in Panama, no full-fledged symphonic orchestra, no established theater groups. That is what happens when the elite does not feel responsible for building a nation because they have not earned it. The same with corporations. You cannot expect to effectively run a corporation with people who have been disenfranchised from it. There will be a lot of foot dragging. This is why the authenticity of the leader, expressed in his deeds and alignment with his utterances, is crucial to effective followership.

From Argentina to Mexico, popular-revolt leaders left us important messages regarding how to lead and manage Latin Americans. Still, it does not mean that those popular revolts held all the answers. The disparity in organizational competencies became all-apparent when our itinerant gauchos witnessed the confrontation between Mexicans and Americans, as in General Pershing's Punitive Expedition. Then, the United States was toying with a motorized force, with airplanes, and with gunboats while Pancho Villa was still moving on horseback and rails, despite the United States having been colonized almost a century later than Mexico.

At its origins, the differences may not be all about management, perhaps not even about leadership alone, but the path must be broken with imagination and audacity, and the best leaders and managers must soon realize that path dependency may be a curse rather than a course, in that it holds Latin America back. The best path may be the one that selectively adds missing competencies to indigenous leadership and people management skills.

# Glossary

| | |
|---|---|
| aficionado | Fan, enthusiast. |
| aide-de-camp | Personal assistant of a senior military officer. |
| ancien | Régime Old Order, frequently alluding to before the French Revolution |
| banderilla | Beribboned barbed dart that the matador thrusts onto the back of the bull as proof of proximity. |
| caudillo | Someone with political power usually exercised in an authoritarian style. |
| carbonari | Early nineteenth-century Italian network of revolutionary societies. |
| chiripá | Rectangular woolen fabric worn between the thighs and hung from the waist. Also used rolled up on the forearm to shield from knife blows. |
| criollo | Demonym attributed to the locally born from Iberian peninsular stock. |
| estancia | Ranch usually devoted to rearing cattle and horses. |
| facón | Long knife used by gauchos for fighting and carving. |
| garriadas | Portuguese-style bullfight in which men seek to immobilize the bull with their bare hands. |
| gaucho | Southern Pampa's version of the American cowboy. |
| guapo | Defiant, provocative male. |

guichet — Window where attendant dispenses information; frequently deals with money.

honor — Good reputation.

honores — Tribute with which someone's good reputation is recognized.

kebab — Meat cuts threaded on a skewer.

macho — Strong, vigorous, brave man.

machete — Thin, long knife with one-sided blade; heavy enough to open one's way through thick vegetation.

Maragato — Descendant from inhabitants of Maragataria, in the province of León, Spain.

matador — Bullfighter, responsible for killing the bull if he or she can.

mate — Infusion of the dried leaves of a plant (ilex paraguariensis) indigenous to the River Plate basin.

montonera — Gaucho attacking pack.

patrón — Boss, though in Spanish the noun's meaning is somewhat closer to that of a slave driver.

picador — In a bullfight, the rider who thrusts a lance on the bull's neck to diminish its capacity to lift its head.

saladero — A slaughterhouse where meat was cured by drying and salting.

terroir — Area recognized to be bound by shared cultural traditions that yield a sense of belonging to those familiar with them.

Vizcacha — Small rodent; in *El Gaucho Martin Fierro*, it is the nickname of a person "not to be born on account of the damage he did."

# References


Adam, T. (2005). *Germany and the Americas: Culture, politics, and history.* Santa Barbara, CA: ABC-CLIO.

Aguilar, H. C. & Meyer, L. (1993). *In the shadow of the Mexican revolution.* Dallas: Texas University Press.

Alexander, J. C. (2005). *The meanings of social life: A Cultural Sociology.* Oxford: Oxford University Press.

Alloyn, B. J., Blight, J. G., & Welch, D. A. (1989). "Essence of revision: Moscow, Havana, and the Cuban Missile Crisis."*International Security,* 14(3), 136–172.

Almeida de, M. V. (1996). *The hegemonic male: Masculinity in a Portuguese town.* Providence & Oxford: Berghahn Books.

Antonakis, J. (2003). "Why 'emotional intelligence' does not predict leadership effectiveness: A comment on Prati, Douglas, Ferris, Ammeter, and Buckley," *International Journal of Organizational Analysis,* 11(4), 355–361.

Banco de la República de Colombia. (2017). Sociedad Colombo-Alemana de Transportes Aéreos. http://www.banrepcultural.org/category/autor-institucional/sociedad-colombo-alemana-de-transportes-reos. Accessed on February 6, 2017.

Barton, C. A. (1989)."The scandal of the arena," *Representations,* no. 27.

Bass, B. M., Avolio, B. J., & Atwater, L. (1996). "The transformational and transactional leadership of men and women." *International Review of Applied Psychology,* 45, 5–34.

Bass, B. M., & Steidlmeier, P. (1999). "Ethics, character, and authentic transformational leadership behavior."*Leadership Quarterly,* 10, 181–217.

Bataille, G. (1962). *Erotism: Death and sensuality.* San Francisco: City Light Books.

Bataille, G. (1979). *Histoire de l'Oeil.* Paris: Gallimard.

Behrens, A. (2008). *Cultura e Administração nas Américas.* São Paulo: Saraiva.

Behrens, A. (2009a). "Coyotes vs. road runners: Managing in the Americas." *Harvard Business Review.* http://blogs.hbr.org/cs/2009/08/coyotes_vs_road_runners_managi.html. Accessed on January 30, 2017.

Behrens, A. (2009b). *Culture and management in the Americas.* Palo Alto, CA: Stanford University Press.

Behrens, A. (2010). "Charisma, paternalism, and business leadership in Latin America." *Thunderbird International Business Review,* 52(1), 21–29.

Behrens, A. (2015). "Beyond West-centrism: The way forward for cross-cultural management in Latin America." In N. Holden, S. Michailova, & S. Tietze (Eds.), *The Routledge companion to cross-cultural management* (pp. 208–217). London: Routledge.

Behrens, A., & Wright, J. T. C. (2010). "Human resource management techniques fit poorly in Latin America." In S. Verna (Ed.), *Towards the next orbit: Acorporate Odyssey* (pp. 285–299). New Delhi: Sage.

Benedetti, M.(2001). *Vientos del Exilio,* 2nd ed. Buenos Aires: Editorial Sudamericana.

Bird, C. (1940). *Social psychology.* New York: Appleton-Century.

Bordelois, I. (1999). *Un triángulo crucial: Borges, Güiraldes y Lugones.* Buenos Aires: Eudeba.

Borges, J. L. (2005). *El Martín Fierro.* Buenos Aires: Emecé.

Boyd, D. (2008). *A Legião Estrangeira.* Coimbra, Portugal: Edições.

Brent, A. (2010). *Cyprian and Roman Carthage.* Cambridge: Cambridge University Press.

Brown, J. (1859). *John Brown and the Harpers Ferry Raid.* http://www.wvculture.org/History/jnobrown.html. Accessed on January 31, 2017.

Bunnell, D. (1972). *A horse with no name,* lyrics. http://www.accessback-stage.com/america/song/song005.htm. Accessed January 31, 2017.

Burghardt Du Bois, E. (1909). *John Brown, a biography.* Armonk, NY: M. E. Sharpe.

Canetti, E. (1962). *Crowds and power.* 1st English ed. London: Victor Gollancz Ltd.

Chasteen, J. C. (1995). *Heroes on horseback: A life and times of the last gaucho caudillos.* Albuquerque: University of New Mexico Press.

Chasteen, J. C. (2001). *Born in blood and fire: A concise history of Latin America.* New York: Norton.

Cherlin, A. J. (1992). *Marriage, divorce, remarriage: Social trends in the United States.* Cambridge, MA: Harvard University Press.

Cherlin, A. J. (2009). *The marriage-go-round: The state of marriage and the family in America today.* New York: Knopf Doubleday.

Cogliser, C. C., & Schriesheim, C. A. (2000). "Exploring work unit context and leader-member exchange: A multi-level perspective."*Journal of Organizational Behavior*, 21, 487–511.

Conge, J. A., & Kanugo, R. N. (1998). *Charismatic leadership in organizations.* Berkeley, CA: Sage.

Conrad, J. (1908). *The Duel.* http://www.gutenberg.org. Accessed on January 26, 2017.

Cunha da, E. (1968). *Os sertões,* Rio de Janeiro: Francisco Alves.

Dana Jr., R. H. (1840). *Two Years Before the Mast and Twenty-Four Years After.* The Harvard Classics. 1909–14 #23. Concluding Chapter. http://www.bartleby.com/23/1003.html. Accessed on January 2, 2017.

Darwin, C. (1948). *Voyages of the Adventure and Beagle, Vol. III ("Maldonado").* London: Colburn.

Dasborough, M. T., & Ashkanasy, N. M. (2003). "Emotion and attribution of intentionality in leader-member relationships." *The Leadership Quarterly,* 13, 615–634.

D'Este, C. (1995). *Patton: A genius for war.* New York: HarperCollins.

De Gaulle, C. (1960). *The edge of the sword.* Vancouver: Criterion Books.

Díaz Espino, O. (2004). *El país creado por Wall Street: La historia prohibida de Panamá y Su Canal.* Barcelona: Destino.

Dirceu, J. (2005). "Desaparecidos: O direito à verdade e à justiça." *Blog do Noblat.* http://noblat.oglobo.globo.com/noticias/noticia/2009/06/desaparecidos-direito-verdade-a-justica-199263.html. Accessed on October 25, 2017.

D'Iribarne, P. (1989). *La logique de l'honneur–gestion des entreprises et traditions nationals.* Paris: Seuil.

Dobke, P. R. (2015). *Caudilhismo, Território E Relações Sociais De Poder: O Caso De Aparício Saraiva Na Região Fronteiriça Entre Brasil E Uruguai (1896–1904).* Master dissertation toward the degree in History at Universidade Santa Maria, Brazil.

Douglass, C. (1984). "Toro muerto vaca es." *American Ethnologist,* 11(2), 242–258.

Douglass, C. B. (1997). *Bulls, bullfighting, and Spanish identities.* Phoenix: University of Arizona Press.

Dreazen, Y. J. (2009). Family seeks honors for soldiers who committed suicide. *The Wall Street Journal.* November 25. https://www.wsj.com/articles/SB125911318179763359. Accessed on February 1, 2017.

Duff Gordon, L., Lamping, C., & Alby, F. A. (1845). *The French in Algiers: I. The soldier of the Foreign Legion.* Translated by Lady Lucie Duff Gordon. London: Murray, 1845. Also at https://archive.org/details/frenchinalgierss00duffuoft. Accessed on January 2, 2017.

Dylan, B. (1965). *Like a rolling stone,* lyrics (Highway 61 Revisited, Columbia Records).

Fast, H. (1951). *Spartacus.* Armonk, NY: M. E. Sharp.

Felfe, J., & Schyns, B. (2006). "Personality and the perception of transformational leadership: The impact of extraversion, neuroticism, personal need for structure, and occupational self-efficacy." *Journal of Applied Social Psychology,* 36(3), 708–739.

Fernández, I., Paez, D., & González, J. L. (2005). "Independent and interdependent self-construals and socio-cultural factors in 29 nations." *Revue Internationale de Psychologie Sociale,* 18(1–2), 35–63.

Fiedler, F. E. (1978). "The contingency model and the dynamics of the leadership process." In L. Berkowitz (Ed.), *Advances in experimental social psychology* (Vol. 11, pp. 59–112). New York: Academic Press.

Friede, R. (2015)."As violações dos direitos humanos na defesa nacional e a CNV." *A Defesa Nacional,* 103(828), 19–29.

Fox, J. (2017). "Low-pay jobs boom in the slaughterhouse." *Bloomberg View,* January 6. https://www.bloomberg.com/view/articles/2017-01-06/low-pay-jobs-boom-in-the-slaughterhouse. Accessed on January 7, 2017.

Fuentes, C. (1999). *The buried mirror.* Boston, MA: Houghton Mifflin Books.

Fuentes, F. (1934). *El Compadre Mendoza,* film. http://www.imdb.com/title/tt0023902/. Accessed on January 30, 2017.

Gallant, T. W. (2002). "Honor, masculinity and ritual knife fighting in nineteenth-century Greece." *The American Historical Review,* 105(2), xvi+359–382.

Garibaldi, G., & Dumas, A. (1861). *Garibaldi: An autobiography.* Translated by William Robson. London: Routledge.

Gielow, I. (2008). "Entrevista ao general Nikolai S. Leonov." *No Caderno Mais! da Folha de S. Paulo,* January 13, 5.

Gil Amate, V. (2012). "*Campaña en el Ejército Grande": La Lucha de Domingo F. Sarmiento Contra el Caudillismo.* http://www.cervantesvirtual.com/nd/ark:/59851/bmc25263. Accessed on January 19, 2017.

Gilly, A. (Ed.). (2008). *Felipe Ángeles en la revolución.* México City: Biblioteca Era.

Gilmore, D. D. (1982). "Anthropology of the Mediterranean area." *Annual Review of Anthropology,* 11, 175–205.

Goffee, R., & Jones, G. (2006). *Why should anyone be led by you? What it takes to be an authentic leader.* Cambridge, MA: Harvard Business Press.

Goleman, D., & Boyatzis, R. (2008). "Social intelligence and the biology of leadership." *Harvard Business Review,* 86(9), 74–81.

Goodman, S. (2009). "Poor Mexico, so far from God, so close to the United States."*The WorldPost*, April 1. http://www.huffingtonpost.com/sandy-goodman/poor-mexico-so-far-from-g_b_170899.html. Accessed on February 1, 2017.

Gore, E. (2009). "Los 31 secretos del (anti) management."http://materiabiz.com/los-31-secretos-del-anti-management/. Accessed on January 19, 2017.

Gossett, A. H. (1883).*Translation of Spinoza's (1667) TRACTATUS POLITICUS*. London: G. Bell & Son. Available at https://ebooks.adelaide.edu.au/s/spinoza/benedict/political/. Accessed on January 2, 2017.

Güiraldes, R. (1926). *Don Segundo Sombra*. San Antonio de Areco: Proa.

Halton, B. (2009). "Pioneering matador known as 'The Blond Goddess.' " *Washington Post*, February 20. http://www.washingtonpost.com/wp-dyn/content/article/2009/02/19/AR2009021903183.html. Accessed on January 27, 2017.

Hanson, V. D. (1999). *The soul of battle: From ancient times to the present day, how three great liberators vanquished tyranny*. Washington, DC: Free Press.

Harding, L. (2016). "What are the Panama Papers? A guide to history's biggest data leak."*The Guardian*, April 5. https://www.theguardian.com/news/2016/apr/03/what-you-need-to-know-about-the-panama-papers. Accessed on February 3, 2017.

Hemingway, E. (1932). *Death in the afternoon*. New York: Charles Scribner's Sons.

Hernández, J. (1936).*The gaucho Martin Fierro*. New York: Farrar & Rinehart.

Hernández, J. (1983). *El gaucho Martín Fierro: La vuelta de Martín Fierro*. Volume 66 (11th edition). Buenos Aires: Biblioteca EDAF.

Hernández, J. (2005). *El gaucho Martin Fierro*. Release Date: January 23, 2005. http://www.gutenberg.org/files/14765/14765–8.txt. Accessed on January 2, 2017.

Hetland, H., & Sandal, G. M. (2003). "Transformational leadership in Norway: Outcomes and personality correlates."*European Journal of Work and Organizational Psychology*, 12(2), 147–170.

Hetland, H., Sandal, G. M., & Johnsen, T. (2008) "Followers' personality and leadership."*Journal of Leadership & Organizational Studies*, 14(4), 322–331.

Hitchens, C. (2001). *The trial of Henry Kissinger*. New York: Verso.

Hoschschild, A. (2009). "Americans step in and out or relationships faster than couples in Europe, Japan and Australia."*New York Times*,

*Sunday Book Review*, October 16. http://www.nytimes.com/2009/10/18/books/review/Hochschild-t.html?pagewanted=2. Accessed on January 29, 2017.

Hoshschild, A. (2009). "The state of culture, class and family." *New York Times Review*, October 18. http://www.nytimes.com/2009/10/18/books/review/Hochschild-t.html. Accessed on February 6, 2017.

House, R. J. (1971). "A path-goal theory of leader effectiveness." *Administrative Science Quarterly*, 16, 321–338.

House, R. J., Hanges, P. J., Javidan, P. M., Dorfman, W., & Gupta, V. (Eds.). (2004). *Culture, leadership and organizations: The GLOBE study of 62 societies.* Thousand Oaks, CA: Sage.

Howells, L. T. & S. Becker, W. (1962). "Seating arrangement and leadership emergence."*Journal of Abnormal and Social Psychology*, 64, 148–150.

Humphrey, R. H. (2002). "The many faces of emotional leadership."*The Leadership Quarterly*, 13, 493–504.

Iglesias, W. (2015) in Clarin, Buenos Aires newspaper. "Abdón Porte, el ídolo que se suicidó en el campo de juego." July 1, http://www.clarin.com/futbol/futbolista-suicido-campo-juego_0_Sk7cA85w7e.html. Accessed on July 17, 2017.

Jerome, R. (2001). *Conceptions of postwar German masculinity.* Albany: State University of New York Press.

Kapuściński, R. (1992). *The soccer war.* William Brand (Trans.). London: Vintage.

Kapuściński, R. (2001). *Another day of life.* London: Penguin.

Katz, F. (1998). *The life and times of Pancho Villa.* Palo Alto, CA: Stanford University Press.

Katzenbach, J. R., & Smith, D. K. (1993). "The discipline of teams."*Harvard Business Review*, 71, 111–120.

Klann, G. (2006). *Building character: Strengthening the heart of good leadership.* Hoboken, NJ: John Wiley and Sons.

Krauze, E. (1998). *Mexico: Biography of power.* New York: HarperCollins Publishers.

Kurosawa, A. (1957).*Throne of blood*, film.http://www.imdb.com/title/tt0050613/. Accessed on January 19, 2017.

Kyle, D. G. (1998). *Spectacles of death in Ancient Rome.* London: Routledge.

Lawrence, T.E. (1922). *Seven pillars of wisdom.* https://ebooks.adelaide.edu.au/l/lawrence/te/seven/. Accessed on January 30, 2017.

Leavitt, H. J. (1951). "Some effects of certain communication patterns on group performance." *Journal of Abnormal and Social Psychology*, 46, 38–50.

Lemaitre, R. E. (1980). *Panamá y Su Separación de Colombia.* Bogotá: Pluma.

Lemaitre, R. E. (2003). *Panamá y Su Separación de Colombia.* Bogotá: Intermedio Editores.

Levinson, H. (1973). "Asinine attitudes toward motivation." *Harvard Business Review*, 1(1), 70–76.

Lewin, K., Lewin, R., Lippitt, R., & White K. (1939). "Patterns of aggressive behavior in experimentally created social climates." *Journal of Social Psychology*, 10, 271–299.

Lewin, K., & Lippitt, R. (1938). "An experimental approach to the study of autocracy and democracy: A preliminary note." *Sociometry*, 1, 292–300.

Machado, P. P. (2007). *Lideranças do contestado*. Campinas: Editora Unicamp.

MacKell, J., & Noel, T. J. (2007). *Brothels, bordellos, and bad girls: Prostitution in Colorado, 1860–1930*. Albuquerque: University of New Mexico Press.

MacLeish, A. (1961). The call of danger, New York: *Life Magazine*, July 14.

Madariaga de, S. (1931). *Englishmen, Frenchmen and Spaniards*. Oxford: Oxford University Press.

Maquiavel, N. (2008). *The prince*. São Paulo: Golden Books.

Mann, R. D. (1959). "A review of the relationship between personality and performance in small groups." *Psychological Bulletin*, 56, 241–270.

March, J., & Augier, M. (2004). "James March on education, leadership and Don Quixote: Introduction and leadership." *Academy of Learning and Education*, 3, 169–173. Available at https://wujianzu.wordpress.com/2008/10/17/james-march-on-education-leadership-and-don-quixote-introduction-and-interview/. Accessed on January 29, 2017.

Martinko, M. J., & Thomson, N. F. (1998). "A synthesis and extension of the Weiner and Kelley attribution models." *Basic and Applied Social Psychology*, 20, 271–284.

Maurer, N., & Yu, C. (2006). "What Roosevelt took: The economic impact of the Panama Canal, 1903–37." *Harvard Business School*, paper 06-041, http://www.hbs.edu/faculty/Publication%20Files/06-041.pdf. Accessed October 25, 2017.

McGovern, G., & Moon, Y. (2007). "Companies and the customers who hate them." *Harvard Business Review*, 85(6), 78–84.

Mitchell, T. J. (1986). "Bullfighting, the ritual origin of scholarly myths." *The Journal of American Folklore*, 99(394), 394–414.

Mozejko, D. (1988). "La Construcción de los héroes nacionales, una lectura semiótica de Juan Santamaría." In E. G. Buchard (Ed.), *Fronteras* (pp. 121–148). Editorial Universidad de Costa Rica.

Murdoch, I., & Conradi, E. P. J. (1997). *Existentialists and mystics: Writings on philosophy and literature*. London: Chatto & Windus.

Namier, Sir Lewis. (1963). *Vanished supremacies: Essays on European history 1812–1918*. New York: Harper & Row.

National Archives-USA. http://www.archives.gov/education/lessons/zimmermann/. Accessed on January 3, 2017.

O'Connor, R. (1961). *Black Jack Pershing*. New York: Doubleday.

Olavarría, J. (2007). *Gómez: Un enigma histórico: Una revisión al fenómeno histórico y político de Juan Vicente Gómez*. Caracas: Fundación Olavarría.

Owen, W. (1936). *The gaucho Martin Fierro*: adapted from the Spanish and rendered into English verse by Walter Owen. New York: Farrar & Rinehart.

Paniagua, C. (1994). "Bullfight: The afición." *Psychoanalytic Quarterly*, 63, 84–100.

Pedro de, M. (1975). "Juan Vicente Gómez y su época." *Film*. Caracas, Venezuela, 1975.

Perón, J. D. (1947). "Speech: Éramos un pequeño país…" https://youtu.be/2yw6X-91S7s. Accesed on January 19, 2017.

Pesante, M. L. (2009). "Slaves, servants and wage earners: Free and unfree labour, from Grotius to Blackstone." *History of European Ideas*, 35(3), 289–320.

Pescosolido, A. T. (2002). "Emergent leaders as managers of group emotion." *The Leadership Quarterly*, 13, 583–599.

Pillai, R., & Meindl, J. R. (1998). "Context and charisma: A 'meso' level examination of the relationship of organic structure, collectivism, and crisis to charismatic leadership." *Journal of Management*, 24, 643–671.

Pitt-Rivers, J. (1993). "The Spanish bullfight and kindred activities." *Anthropology Today*, 9(4),11–15.

Primera Plana. (1971). Borges – Simon, detrás del laberinto. (Diálogo entre Herbert Simon y Jorge Luis Borges). http://www.magicasruinas.com.ar/revistero/esto/revdesto140.htm. Accessed on December 8, 2017.

Roberts, C. J. (2008). Dissenting Supreme Court of the United States https://www.law.cornell.edu/supct/html/07-552.ZD.html. Accessed on January 2, 2017.

Ruwhiu, D., & Elkin, G. (2016). "Converging pathways of contemporary leadership: In the footsteps of Mãori and servant leadership." *Leadership*, 12(3), 308–323.

Samovar, L. A., Porter, R. E., & McDaniel, E. R. (2009). *Communication between cultures*. Wadsworth series in speech communication. Boston, MA: Cengage Learning.

Sarmiento, D. F. (1852). Sud América. Vol. II. Santiago, Julio 17 de 1851. As portrayed in *Campaña en el ejército grande, aliado de Sud América*. Campaña In *El Ejército Grande, Aliado De Sud América*. Teniente Coronel Domingo F. Sarmiento. Primera Entrega. Río De Janeiro: Imprenta Imp. Y Const. De J. Villeneuve Y C.

Sarmiento, D. F.. (2000). *Vida de Juan Facundo Quiroga.* Benito Varela Jácome (Ed.). Biblioteca Virtual Miguel de Cervantes. http://www.cervantesvirtual.com/servlet/SirveObras/01474062099103040832268/index.htm. Accessed on October 25, 2017

Sashkin, M. (1988). "The visionary leader." In J. A. Conger & R. N. Kanugo (Eds.), *Charismatic leadership: The elusive factor in organizational effectiveness* (pp. 122–160). San Francisco: Josey-Bass.

Sashkin, M. (2004). "Transformational leadership approaches: A review and synthesis." In J. Antonakis, A. Cianciolo, & R. J. Sternberg (Eds.), *The nature of leadership* (pp. 171–196). Thousand Oaks, CA: Sage.

Saunders, G. E. (1981). "Men and women in Southern Europe: A review of some aspects of cultural complexity." *Journal of Psychoanalytic Anthropology*, 4, 413–434.

Schama, S. (2010). *The American future: A history.* New York: HarperCollins.

Schneider, J. (1971). "Of vigilance and virgins: Honor, shame and access to resources in Mediterranean societies." *Ethnology*, 10(1), 1–24.

Schyns, B., Felfe, J., & Blank, H. (2007). "Is charisma hyper-romanticism? Empirical evidence from new data and a meta-analysis." *Applied Psychology: An International Review*, 56(4), 505–527.

Schyns, B., & Sanders, K. (2007). "In the eyes of the beholder: Personality and the perception of leadership." *Journal of Applied Social Psychology*, 37(10), 2345–2363.

Scorsese, M. (1980).*Raging bull.* Film. http://www.imdb.com/title/tt0081398/. Accessed on November 24, 2017.

Scott, R. (1977). *The Duelists.* Film. http://www.imdb.com/title/tt0075968/. Accessed on January 27, 2017.

Shakespeare, W. (c1599). *Henry V.* http://shakespeare.mit.edu/henryv/henryv.4.3.html. Accessed on January 7, 2017.

Shakespeare, W. (c1606). *The Tragedy of Macbeth.* http://shakespeare.mit.edu/macbeth/full.html. Accessed on January 7, 2017.

Shartle, C. L. (1951). "Studies of naval leadership." In H. Guetzkow (Ed.), *Group, Leadership and Men* (pp. 119–133). Pittsburgh, PA: Carnegie Press.

Sinclar, U. (1906). *The jungle.* New York: Doubleday, Jabber & Company.

Slattery, M. T. (1982). *Felipe Angeles and the Mexican revolution.* Richmond, VA: Prinit Press.

Small, S., Westwell, I., & Westwood, J. (2002). *Home fronts, technologies of war: History of World War I* (Vol. 3). Singapore: Marshall Cavendish Corporation.

Sobel, B. (1997). *The fighting Pattons.* Westport, CT: Greenwood Publishing Group.

Soto, B. "Riding through hell." In *Coming from the Sky.* Berlin: Noise Records. Lyrics at http://www.metrolyrics.com/riding-through-hell-lyrics-heavenly.html. Accessed on January 3, 2017.

Spinoza, B. (1667). *Tratactus politicus.* http://users.telenet.be/rwmeijer/spinoza/works.htm. Accessed on January 30, 2017.

Spinoza, B. (1883). *Political treatise (tractatus politicus).* A. H. Gossett (Trans.). London: G. Bell & Son. https://ebooks.adelaide.edu.au/s/spinoza/benedict/political/. Accessed on January 2, 2017.

Stogdill, R. M. (1948). "Personal factors associated with leadership: A survey of the literature." *Journal of Psychology*, 25, 35–71.

Suárez, J. I. (1991). "Portugal's 'Saudosismo' movement: An esthetics of Sebastianism." *Luso-Brazilian Review*, 28(1), 129–140.

Tal, D., & Avishag, G. (2015). "Charisma research, knowledge growth and disciplinary shifts: A holistic view." *Society*, 52(4), 351–359.

Talbert, R. (2008). *Negative intelligence: The army and the American Left, 1917 to 1941.* Jackson: University Press of Mississippi.

Tamás, G. (2011). "Path dependency and path creation in a strategic perspective." *Journal of Futures Studies*, 15(4), 93–108.

*The Economist.* (1879). "The Panama Canal (Jul. 26th)." http://www.economist.com/node/15006640. Accessed on January 31, 2017.

Thompson, N. (1990). "The uses of adversity." In N. Gash (Ed.), *Wellington: Studies in the military and political career of the First Duke of Wellington* (pp. 1–10). Manchester: Manchester University Press.

Toynbee, A. J. (1987). *A study of history.* Volumes 7–10. Oxford: Oxford University Press.

Uhl-Bien, M. (2003). "Relationship development as a key ingredient for leadership development." In S. E. Murphy & R. E. Riggio (Eds.), *The future of leadership development* (pp. 129–147). Mahwah, NJ: Lawrence Erlbaum.

Uhl-Bien, M., Graen, G. B., & Scandura, T. A. (2000). "Implications of leader-member exchange (LMX) for strategic human resource management systems: relationships as social capital for competitive advantage."*Research in Personnel and Human Resources Management*, 18, 137–185.

Uhl-Bien, M., Marion, R., & McKelvey, B. (2007). "Complexity leadership theory: Shifting leadership from the Industrial Age to the Knowledge Era."*Leadership Quarterly*, 18, 298–318.

United States Armory and Arsenal at Harper's Ferry. http://www.civilwar.org/education/history/biographies/john-brown.html. Accessed on January 3, 2017.

Valerio, A. (2001). *Anita Garibaldi: A biography.* Santa Barbara, CA: Praeger.

Vázquez, L. (2008). "Cipriano Castro, 100 años de actualidad." Producción Villa del cine. http://bit.ly/63hDvV. Accessed on October 25, 2017.

Velásquez, R. J. (1978).*Confidencias Imaginárias de Juan Vicente Gómez.* Film. Caracas: Teura, 14th edition – 2008.

Vroom, V. H., & Jago, A. G. (1998). "Situation effects and levels of analysis in the study of leaders participation." In F. Yammarino & F. Dansereau (Eds.), *Leadership: The multi-level approaches* (pp. 145–159). New York: JAI.

Welsome, E. (2007). *The General and the Jaguar: Pershing's hunt for Pancho Villa: A true story of revolution and revenge.* Lincoln: University of Nebraska Press.

Wilcox, R. (2010). *Target: Patton – The plot to assassinate General George S. Patton.* Washington, DC: Regenery.

Windrow, M., & Roffe, M. (1971). *French Foreign Legion. Book 17 of Men-At-Arms Series.* London: Osprey Publishing.

Yukl, G. (1998). *Leadership in organizations.* New York: Prentice-Hall.

Zimmerman Telegram. (1907). *Teaching with Documents: The Zimmermann Telegram.* http://www.archives.gov/education/lessons/zimmermann. Accessed October 25, 2017.

Zorrilla de San Martín, J. (1960). *Tabaré.* Volumen 36 de Colección Estrada. Montevideo: Ángel Estrada.

# Index

# Index

www.ingramcontent.com/pod-product-compliance
Lightning Source LLC
Chambersburg PA
CBHW060817310726
48980CB00002B/325

* 9 7 8 1 7 8 3 0 8 7 1 0 5 *